Guerrilla Music Marketing Online

129 Free and Low-Cost Strategies to Promote and Sell Your Music on the Internet

Bob Baker

Spotlight Publications
St. Louis, MO

www.TheBuzzFactor.com

Guerrilla Music Marketing Online

Published by Spotlight Publications and TheBuzzFactor.com
PO Box 28441, St. Louis, MO 63146 USA
(314) 963-5296 • bob@bob-baker.com

ISBN-10: 0-9714838-7-6
ISBN-13: 978-0-9714838-7-3

Printed in the United States of America.

Disclaimer

This book is designed to provide information on marketing, promoting, and selling music. It is sold with the understanding that the publisher and author are not engaged in rendering legal, accounting, or other professional services. If legal or other expert assistance is required, the services of a competent professional should be sought.

It is not the purpose of this book to cover the full range of information that is otherwise available on this topic, but instead to complement, amplify, and supplement other texts. You are urged to read all available material and tailor the information to your individual needs.

Every effort has been made to make this book as accurate as possible. However, there may be mistakes, and with all the rapid changes online in particular, some details may be inaccurate by the time you read this. Therefore, this text should be used only as a general guide and not as the ultimate source of information on the topic.

The author and publisher shall have neither liability nor responsibility to any person or entity with respect to any loss or damage caused, or alleged to have been caused, directly or indirectly, by the information contained in this book.

Dedicated to YOU – the independent artist who has gifts and talents to share with the world!

Get your free *Music Marketing Secrets* report

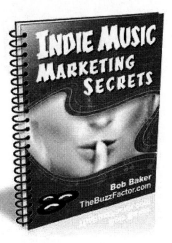

Congratulations on acquiring this book and investing the time to read it and put its many ideas and resources to good use.

But it's only a first step.

That's why you are encouraged to visit **www.TheBuzzFactor.com** right now and download a free copy of Bob Baker's special report called *Indie Music Marketing Secrets*.

It's packed full of even more free and low-cost guerrilla marketing ideas that will help you get more exposure, attract more fans, and sell more music and merchandise than ever before.

If you're an independent songwriter or musician – or if you manage a band or small record label – **please take a minute to go there now and get FREE access to some of Bob's most potent music marketing tips**.

The *Indie Music Marketing Secrets* special report is waiting for you now at www.TheBuzzFactor.com.

About the author

Bob Baker is the author of the highly acclaimed *Guerrilla Music Marketing Handbook* and several other books, including *Branding Yourself Online* and *Unleash the Artist Within*. He also developed the "Music Marketing 101" course at Berkleemusic, the online continuing education division of Berklee College of Music.

Bob is an indie musician and former music magazine editor who is dedicated to showing musicians of all kinds how to get exposure, connect with fans, sell more music, and increase their incomes through their artistic passions.

Since 1995 Bob has published "The Buzz Factor" ezine, one of the first music tips email newsletters in existence. He was one of the early proponents of musicians taking their careers into their own hands and not relying on major record labels or industry gatekeepers to save them. Bob is on a mission to empower artists using his articles, ezine, blog, podcast and video clips.

Visit **www.TheBuzzFactor.com** for more details.

Contents

Images on the cover and many throughout the book come from Stock.XCHNG at www.sxc.hu.

Introduction

The Internet. It's huge – and growing all the time. The really good news for musicians is that millions of people go online every day to search for and purchase music.

Let's take a quick look at the music slice of the online pie. According to the IFPI Digital Music Report:

- Global digital music sales reached approximately $4.6 billion USD in 2010.

- About 29% of all recorded music industry revenues worldwide now come from digital channels (which include download stores, subscription services, streaming sites, and mobile phone access).

- Single track downloads in the U.S. totaled more than 1.1 billion paid song purchases in 2010.

- Digital album sales grew to 86.3 million units in 2010, accounting for more than 26% of all U.S. album sales (Nielsen SoundScan).

- iTunes, the dominant player in the digital music market, crossed the 10 billion download sales milestone in February 2010.

And that's just the traditional music business. There's also a lot of action taking place under the radar on independent music sites. For instance, since 1998, indie music site CD Baby has sold several million physical and digital albums online to customers and paid more than

$177 million directly to artists. Not too shabby. No doubt, there's a lot of music buying and selling going on in cyberspace!

Now for the Bad News ...

The Internet can seem overwhelming and mysterious to a lot of people – including tech-savvy musicians. There are so many options and only so much time and money to invest in them.

The solution: Embrace a guerrilla music marketing mindset!

What is that? Well, it's a way of thinking and a manner of approaching your music career that allows you to be immensely effective using your creativity and brain power instead of having to rely on cash and clout.

I've written about it many times before in my bestselling *Guerrilla Music Marketing Handbook* and the follow-up book *Guerrilla Music Marketing: Encore Edition.* Jay Conrad Levinson has been writing about it to a general audience for decades in his wonderful series of *Guerrilla Marketing* books.

This is the third in my series of *Guerrilla Music Marketing* books – with this title focusing exclusively on the many free and low-cost ways you can use the Internet to promote your music, reach fans, make money, and leave a lasting musical legacy.

If you're not familiar with the principles of guerrilla marketing, here are just some of the highlights:

- Guerrillas don't believe a big budget is necessary for success. They don't use a lack of money as an excuse. They use their *creativity* instead of cash and their *brains* instead of their bank accounts.

- Guerrilla music marketers aren't stuck in the traditional ways of the past. They do more than think outside the box. As my friend Nancy Moran says, they "crush the box" and are open to creating entirely new ways to get exposure and connect with fans.

- Guerrillas know that the best way to promote themselves is to be authentic and genuine. Effective marketing is not about being bold, brash and "in your face" (unless that's truly who you are). The best marketing tactics will cater to your strengths and personality. You won't have to pretend you're someone you're not.

- Guerrillas also know that marketing shouldn't be a dreadful chore or a "necessary evil." When done right, it can be extremely creative, playful and fun – which is the opposite of how most musicians approach it.

Bottom line: When it comes to Internet music marketing, embrace a guerrilla attitude. Don't be intimidated. You don't have to compete with the big players to be successful. Just take it one step at a time.

Look over the many simple ideas in this book and start implementing them. Try out a couple at first, then a few more. Before you know it, you'll be creating a buzz and attracting attention to your music and to yourself online.

Are you ready to get cracking?

Good. Let's dive in!

Laying the Foundation for Online Music Promotion

In this first section, we examine 12 key principles that are crucial to laying the groundwork for everything you'll do to promote your music online. So be sure to keep these in mind as you craft your Internet marketing plans.

#1

Ready, Aim, Fire! – Know Where Your Target Is

It's a big world out there – especially on the Internet. The number of Internet users worldwide is now nearly 2 billion people. That's right. Billion with a B. More than 265 million of those users are in North America alone. It's intimidating to think about connecting with all those people. No wonder so many musicians get frustrated and feel overwhelmed when it comes to promoting themselves online.

Have no fear. You don't have to reach all those people. You don't even have to reach all music fans online. If you try, you'll never reach your goals and will curse me and anyone who's ever been associated with the Internet – including Al Gore.

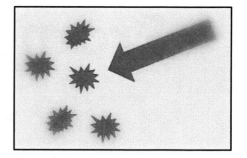

To successfully promote yourself online, you need to start a relationship with only a small sliver of the total number of people online. Think about these numbers: If you could reach just one-hundredth of one percent (0.01%) of those 2 billion people, you'd have 200,000 potential fans. That's a lot of people!

Bottom line: Don't try to be all things to all people. Don't attempt to reach a wide section of the online population. It's not all about huge numbers and how many friends and followers you have. Your objective is to focus your limited time and energy on the web sites, blogs, social media sites, and online forums where the people most likely to be attracted to your music hang out.

Got it? Good.

#2

Focus on the Most Important Factor That Determines Your Success

Musicians venture onto the Web for all sorts of reasons. Some put up a web site just because everybody else is doing it or because they think it's the best way to impress industry people. Others establish an Internet presence because they think search engines will list their site and drive traffic to it while they sleep.

What's the real reason *you* should promote yourself online? Here's my best answer, and you should apply this concept to just about every action you take to promote your music, online and off:

Your main focus should be to attract your ideal listener and turn them into fans, then nurture your relationships with a growing number of them.

No other factor will influence your level of success like a large and enthusiastic fan base. It doesn't matter how impressive your record label, attorney, manager, publicist, or radio promotions person is. None of that means squat if fans don't connect with you. However, you can have no label deal, attorney, manager, etc., and still be a huge success if you have fans – and lots of them.

Fans are the only thing that counts (along with the quality of your music and your integrity), so put a priority on courting them. Use the unique interactive qualities of the Web to communicate with people interested in your music. Get to know them. Allow them to get to

11

know you and the intimate details that led you to create the music they enjoy so much.

Forget all the hype and distractions and put your focus where it needs to be the most: on fans!

#3

Develop a Web "Presence" – Not Just a Web Site

When many novice music promoters think of Internet marketing, they believe it's all about putting up a web site and then driving traffic to it by buying banner ads and getting a lot of good reviews about the latest album.

Sure, those are two possible ways to promote your music online. But if you limit yourself to those options, you'll miss a world of opportunity.

Another line of faulty reasoning is thinking that online music promotion is about search engine optimization (SEO). If you only did well in search results, your worries would be over. It's true that putting basic SEO principles into practice can be helpful. But it's still not the ultimate solution.

Key: The best way to promote and sell your music online is to think beyond your own web site.

Make no mistake, you need an attractive and well-organized site (and I'll cover my top tips in that area soon). But to make a real impact as a musician, songwriter or band, you need much more than a good web site ...

You Need a Web Presence!

But what do I mean by "presence"?

You have a strong presence online when a growing number of people who have an interest in your genre keep finding you in the places where they spend time online.

Sure, doing well in Google searches for your ideal words and phrases is one important part of having an Internet presence. But there's so much more to it.

Having a Web presence also means that your name, album titles, and song samples appear on prominent sites that cater to your musical style. It means your name keeps popping up on music review sites, blogs, podcasts, and active discussion forums related to your genre.

You also expand your presence when music fans find you on Facebook, Twitter, YouTube, LinkedIn, and any number of other social networking sites. It grows when people who subscribe to your email updates forward your latest message to their friends.

You further establish your presence by starting your own blog or podcast, while also making comments on other people's blogs and podcasts. It expands again when you do text, audio and video interviews online.

Key point: You set yourself up for success by making sure you can be found in multiple places where your ideal listeners and fans hang out online.

That's what I mean by developing a Web presence. And that's exactly what this book will help you do.

#4

Register a Memorable Domain Name

As you may know, a domain name is your address on the Internet. It is what people type into a web browser to find you online. Yahoo.com,

NPR.org, and EarthLink.net are all examples of domain names. As a self-promoting musician, you need one too.

Domain names are pretty easy to get. You simply use a domain name registrar, which is a company authorized to assign domain names. The whole transaction takes place online. Here are three domain name registrar sites (with rates ranging from roughly $9 to $15 a year):

GoDaddy
www.godaddy.com

DirectNic
www.directnic.com

Buy Domains
www.buydomains.com

When you're on one of these sites, you can search for available domain names. Just type in a name you want and hit the submit button. The service will let you know right away if the name is available as a .com, .net, .org, and more.

Tip: I recommend you find a name that is available as a .com address. It's too hard to train people to type .net and the others.

The best way to start searching is to use your actual name or your band name. If you are John Smith, then JohnSmith.com would be ideal. If you formed the Motley Blues Band, then MotleyBluesBand.com would be perfect.

If the domain name you want is already taken, see if you can add another word, especially if it's related to your genre, such as:

```
JohnSmithBlues.com
JohnSmithMusic.com
MotleyBluesMusic.com
MotleyBluesBandOnline.com
```

Key: The trick is to choose a domain name that is memorable, easy to spell, and relates directly to what your band or music is about.

For instance, BlagojevichReggaeMusic.com is a weak domain name. There are too many ways to misspell it. But IslandMusicOnline.com has a fighting chance of being remembered and typed into a web browser correctly.

You may think all of the good .com domain names are taken. But you might be surprised by how many good ones are still left. If you haven't already done so, go claim yours today!

(Note: We'll cover how to design your web site for maximum impact in Section Two.)

#5

Set Up Your Email and Signature File

Once you have a domain name registered, you should set up an email account associated with it. In other words, on your web site and business cards, you want people to contact you using an address like John@MotleyBluesBand.com – NOT JohnMBB@hotmail.com. Using one of the free email services as your calling card shouts out "amateur!" So take the extra step to use an email address associated with your domain name.

There are many ways to do this, depending on your web host and whether you use Outlook or some other program. I highly recommend Google's Gmail at mail.google.com.

I simply have my incoming email forwarded to my Gmail account. Yes, Gmail is a free service, but the cool thing about it is that you can adjust the settings so your outgoing messages come from you@yourdomain (in my case, bob@thebuzzfactor.com).

Another thing you should do is create a "signature file," which is a small bit of descriptive and informative text that is added to the bottom of every email message you send. This is a simple but highly effective marketing tool, because it allows you to reinforce your musical identity and contact info with every email you send.

Want an example? Here's the sig file that musician Ian Narcisi uses:

```
Ian Narcisi
Progressive rock indie musician
Singer/songwriter, drummer, keyboardist

http://ianmusic.com/
http://iannarcisi.blogspot.com/
http://myspace.com/ianmuzic
http://twitter.com/IanNarcisi
```

If you're not using an email sig file yet, create one and start using it now!

#6

Build Your #1 Marketing Asset

Guess what I've found to be the strongest music promotion and sales tool?

MySpace? iTunes? Media exposure? Nope.

The #1 music marketing asset that any artist can have is a mailing list. That's right, it's the number of people who have willingly given you their name and email address and, in essence, have said, "Hey, I'm interested in your music and what you stand for. I'd like more information, so keep me posted."

Key point: If you want to promote yourself effectively online, you need to start building a mailing list of people interested in you and your music. And start doing it yesterday!

Without a growing list, you become a passive music promoter who sits on the sidelines and hopes that people respond to the messages you put out. But *with* a mailing list, you become a proactive marketer who controls the flow of information directly to the people who need it the most: your potential buyers and fans.

Publishing an email newsletter (also known as an ezine) is not the exhausting chore that some make it out to be. The biggest first step is deciding what service you want to use to manage your email database and delivery.

If you happen to have an account at **ReverbNation** (www.reverbnation.com), **Bandzoogle** (www.tinyurl.com/cbye78), or **HostBaby** (www.hostbaby.com), all of them have email list management features.

Here are three more email services specifically for musicians:

BandLetter
www.bandletter.com

FanBridge
www.fanbridge.com

iFanz
www.ifanz.com

And here are four general email newsletter services. The first two are free; the other two are fee-based:

Yahoo Groups
groups.yahoo.com

Google Groups
groups.google.com

Constant Contact
www.constantcontact.com

AWeber
www.aweber.com

Bottom line: Start building a mailing list now!

#7

Gather Email Addresses at Live Shows

One great way to generate ezine subscribers is to use your live shows to build your mailing list. How? Well, the secret is to … *ask people to sign up!* And don't be timid about it. Most acts put a sign-up sheet at their sales table or on the stage and invite people to sign up. But not a whole lot of people will take you up on that offer.

Take an extra step to gather those names and addresses. Some acts put their sign-up sheet on a clipboard and pass it around the room. Others have a friend walk around the venue and kindly ask people to sign up. Bribe people with free candy! Whatever it takes.

Another idea: Have a CD giveaway where people have to fill out a small form and throw it into a bucket. You draw one lucky winner, but the names and addresses of everyone who entered are yours to keep – and add to your mailing list.

#8

Offer Strong Incentives to Subscribe

Another great way to build an email list fast is to pile on a lot of good reasons why people should subscribe. Don't just ask people to sign up for email updates. Who needs more messages clogging their inboxes? Make them feel like they're getting an exclusive "backstage pass." Offer special goodies that are only available to subscribers, such as free MP3 downloads, sneak peeks at your newest songs, special subscriber-only discounts on music, merchandise and tickets, etc.

Example: Seattle musician Scott Andrew asks fans on his web site to "Join the Demo Club to unlock new music, get discounts, tour dates, and other neato stuff."

Notice that Scott is not asking people to sign up to get email. Nobody wants that! So he reframes the request and instead asks them to become "a member" of his Demo Club. Come up with your own spin and create a strong incentive to get on your fan email list too.

#9

Communicate With Your Fans Regularly

Okay, so you've got a mailing list up and running, and new fans are signing up all the time. Congratulations! But you're only halfway done. The second part of the mailing list equation is using it. Yes, you have to communicate with these good people who have an interest in you and your music!

George Howard – the former President of Rykodisc, current manager of Carly Simon, and author of *Music Publishing 101* – once wrote, "The single best tool for converting fans to paying customers is email. While email is an increasingly ineffective tool for communication, it still yields a higher return with respect to sales than any other tool. Therefore it is imperative that you use your email newsletter wisely."

Get the point?

Ideally, you should send something to your list on a regular schedule: once a week, every other week, once a month. I recommend you send something at least monthly – and more often if you can. Whatever you do, don't go long stretches when subscribers don't hear from you at all.

Key: Also, don't let the terms "email newsletter" or "ezine" intimidate you. Email messages to your list don't have to be long. In fact, it's much better if they're short and to the point. People will be more likely to open your emails if they know it won't take a lot of their time.

Your messages will also be more warmly received if you deliver some nugget of value (like a new free download, video commentary, or funny story) along with any sales pitch.

Don't have anything new to say? Sure you do. Point your fans to a cool new music resource you've recently discovered. Make them aware of your media appearances and live events. Share a personal experience that inspired you.

More ideas: Hold a contest or offer a discount. Ask for input on the next song you're recording. Make them aware of other cool new bands and artists you've found that they should know about.

In short, think about the needs of your subscribers and ask yourself, "What's the most helpful thing I can deliver to my fans in a timely manner?"

Then deliver it.

#10

Learn to Communicate Clearly

If you're sold on the advice I've dished out so far, congratulations! You're miles ahead of most indie musicians. From now on you will focus your marketing efforts by going to the places where your ideal fans congregate. Great. But there's a right way and a wrong way to present yourself via these targeted avenues.

One way is to mindlessly announce, "Hey, here I am. Check me out." With this method, you might list a band name and a web site. You also might feel proud of yourself for taking action. Sorry, but you haven't done yourself any favors by doing these things alone. Most fans and industry people who view these types of senseless interruptions think, "Who cares?"

There's a better way.

For starters, when you communicate with anyone online (whether it's an email to a fan, a comment on Facebook, or a pitch to an online music reviewer) you must be clear about who you are, what type of music you play, and what sets you apart from other similar acts.

Why do this? Because once you know where your best potential fans and media sources hang out, you need to make sure that your earliest contact with them lets them know right away that your music is something they'll probably enjoy.

What will help you accomplish that most effectively? Something like ...

"Dude, check out my web site. Just posted some new tracks."?

(Believe it or not, I get a lot of emails like this.)

Or ... Compare that to a message along the lines of ...

"Hi. Love your rockabilly web site. Thought you might be interested in my band, The Roadblasters. We're a rockabilly band that plays original songs about classic cars. We're a big hit in Cincinnati and perform regularly at NASCAR and drag racing events in the region. I'd be happy to send you our new CD, Feels on Wheels, *or you can listen to MP3s on our web site."*

See the advantages of being clear about who you are and what you play? It helps you cut through the chaos and noise online. It allows the people most likely to support you to become interested in you and want to know (and hear) more. Keep this principle in mind whenever you take action to promote yourself on the Internet.

#11

Tap Into the Mind, Body and Soul

To effectively promote yourself on the Internet, you must "sell" yourself. That doesn't mean you have to "sell out" and degrade your integrity. But it does mean you must reach out and communicate who you are and why people should care.

So, what's the best way to do that? How do you get the attention of fans? Do you accomplish that by announcing where you're from, who produced your CD, how many music awards you've won, and what process you used to master your latest recording?

No.

Those details are nice and they may help persuade some people, but most music consumers will become fans for a reason that has nothing to do with the facts and features of your musical product. They will be attracted to you because of the way your music and personality make them feel.

That's right, *feel*.

The most powerful response you can get from someone is based on emotion and the way your music affects them physically and mentally, and sometimes spiritually. Author and speaker Tony Robbins refers to this mysterious phenomenon as a "state change."

Key: Your most hardcore fans will react to your music in a way that makes them feel different (and usually much better) while they listen to your music. Their heart rate and body chemistry will actually shift when they hear your songs. And sometimes, after they know you, the shift may occur when they merely see your picture, hear you speak, or read about you (like a music lover's version of Pavlov's dog).

Your job as an independent self-promoter is to understand the powerful effect your music has, and to use that knowledge to spread those great feelings to even more people.

For example, you could announce:

"We're a four-piece band from Kansas City. Our new CD is getting airplay on 12 stations in the Midwest."

Or ... you could say something more "state change"-oriented like:

"Our blend of rap and rock is for you if you crave an adrenaline rush with a touch of humor. Feel the edge and a good belly laugh at the same time."

See the difference? One is ho-hum and factual; the other speaks directly to how a fan benefits from hearing the music. From now on, always use this "state change" principle to attract more fans.

#12

Employ the Ultimate Secret to Music Success

In these pages I share dozens of effective ways to promote and sell your music online. But you don't have to implement all of these ideas and take all of these steps to be successful. In fact, you shouldn't even try. The worst thing you can do is flip through these pages, declare "There's no way I can do all this stuff and still have a life," and end up doing nothing.

Think of this list as an all-you-can-eat buffet. Sure, you could try to eat everything that's laid out before you. But you shouldn't do that. If you did, you'd stuff yourself and feel bloated and uncomfortable.

Instead, look over what's available to you and make choices. "Oh, I like that. That looks good too. I wouldn't feel right doing *that*. I've never done *that* before, but it might be fun to try."

Also, consider pursuing the ultimate secret to music success ...

Many musicians want to crank up the "hype machine" and talk about launching a big "push" to promote themselves. I understand that line of thinking. They're excited and want to make a splash sooner rather than later.

But the truth is, most success in music builds slowly over time. It takes years of persistence and doing a series of small things on a daily, weekly and monthly basis before you see major signs of progress.

All of these efforts act like layers of paint on an artist's canvas that take form over time. At first, the image is fuzzy and only a handful of people know who you are and what you do. As you continue to spread your message and leave little promotional splashes across the Internet, your notoriety slowly expands and the picture of your musical identity becomes clearer.

Eventually, a multiplying effect takes hold and thousands of people are hearing about you and responding positively.

Insight: The thing is, no one email, song, web site redesign, or music review makes a huge splash by itself. It's the combined effect of all your marketing efforts that builds over time. They are drops in a bucket that turn into a steady trickle and, before you know it, a full-blown waterfall that erupts into a tidal wave.

That's the real secret to music success.

Now get busy reading the rest of this book and start leaving your own promotional crumbs across the Internet!

In the next section we'll cover how to set up the hub of your online operations: your own artist or music company web site. Go to the next page to continue ...

Creating a Highly Effective Artist Web Site

There are so many places and ways to establish an online presence for your music. At the center of all this activity is your own web site. Use the tips in this section to create a site that attracts fans and generates revenue.

#13

Create an Effective Artist Web Site Hub

There are a lot of things you can do to promote and sell music online, as well as a lot of sites where you can set up personal profiles. But the heart of your online activity should be your own artist (or music company) web site.

Don't make the mistake of using your MySpace or Facebook page as your primary Internet real estate. Yes, these are cool free services that are fairly easy to manage. But the big drawback is that you don't really control them. And since they are free, these sites don't owe you anything.

Many bands have had their accounts at these popular sites simply disappear, without explanation. It could happen to you too. And suddenly, you'll find you no longer have access to the friend list you spent so much time building.

Best approach: Use your presence on the many social media sites to funnel fans to your own personal web site, where you control the design, the mailing list, the features, and more. Plus, on your own web site, you don't have to compete with flashing banner ads, thousands of other artists, and a million conversations clamoring for attention.

Great! You're sold on the idea of having your own web site hub. Now you have to create one from scratch or update an existing site. I'll share several solid principles with you over the next few pages to help you do that.

But first you must find a place to "host" your web site. Here are three hosting services specifically for musicians:

Bandzoogle
www.tinyurl.com/cbye78

HostBaby
www.hostbaby.com

Broadjam
www.broadjam.com/hosting

To find a web site designer, check out the **Hostbaby Web Designer Database** at www.hostbaby.com/wddb

For more advice on this topic, take a look at my **Killer Music Web Sites** report at www.bob-baker.com/buzz/music-web-site.html.

#14

Define Your Web Site's Purpose and Goals

Not all musical artists are created equal. That same concept applies to music web sites. Your personal domain on the Web needs to serve two masters: The needs of your fans *AND* your own marketing and music career goals.

To help you define your site's main objectives, ask yourself this key question:

What do I want people to *do, think and feel* when they visit my web site?

Here are some possible answers in the DO category:
- purchase music directly from my site
- sign up for my email list
- listen to my song samples
- watch a music video
- hire me to perform at their venue

Here are some possible THINK goals:
- realize I am a seasoned performer
- understand the type of music I play and how it benefits them
- comprehend what causes I stand for
- find out when and where my live shows are
- discover where my music is available for sale
- know what I look like

Finally, what emotional response do you want to elicit from your visitors? How do you want your web site to make them FEEL?
- empowered and inspired
- sad and melancholy
- turned on and aroused
- outraged and angry
- silly and fun-loving
- relaxed and mellow
- energized and ready to party

Warning: Please don't say you want your web site to accomplish "all of the above." That's asking too much. Prioritize the actions, thoughts and feelings you want your site to evoke.

Most artists and music promoters never consider these important details – to their detriment. You must clarify your web site's *do, think and feel* goals first. Only then can you design a site that will gently lead people to take the actions and think the thoughts that are most important to you.

#15

Make Your Home Page Clear and Easy to Read

Your web site's home page is the welcome mat of your online presence. Don't confuse people and scare them away before they even take their first step inside your personal domain.

Tip: This should be obvious, but just in case it isn't ... Please don't assault people with a dizzying array of bells, whistles, and other nonsense when they visit your home on the Internet.

Don't use Flash intro pages, no matter how much your designer says they're cool. (Flash is a popular multimedia platform that adds animation and interactivity to web pages. It has its place, but can be overused.) And don't make your site too graphic heavy. A music web site can look attractive without overwhelming a visitor's eyes and their web browser's ability to render pages.

Great. You know what not to do. Now, here are several things you should do to make your home page appealing and effective ...

#16

Fit the Most Important Info Into One Screen

The idea here is to avoid long, scrolling pages. That means being ruthlessly terse and pithy with the amount of "stuff" you place on your home page. On interior pages you can get away with more text and content, but resist the urge to tell your entire story right up front. Too much information too soon may actually chase people away – and that won't help you attract more fans and sell your music.

#17

Use Plenty of "White Space"

Along with being selective about the amount of information you initially throw at people, also be kind to your web visitors' eyes. Don't cram too many things too close together. Give your web pages space to breathe. Your readers will thank you and stay longer on your web site when you do.

#18

Make It More Than a Sales Pitch

One of the common web design mistakes I see musicians and record labels make is turning their home page into a giant "Buy Now" button. Sure, you want to let people know you have music for sale. But that's not the sole purpose of having a web site. In addition, your site should be set up to highlight samples of songs, reveal who you are as an artist, inspire people to subscribe to your email updates, and more.

#19

Focus on the Upper Left Corner of the Page

Research has shown that web users look first at the upper left corner of a web page, then work their way down and to the right, in much the same way that most people read text on a printed page. So place your name, photo, or an eye-catching image in this powerful, upper left-hand corner.

#20

Give Visitors "Eye Anchors"

People generally scan most web sites. So don't place lots of long, scrolling text on your pages. Instead, use:

- short paragraphs
- bullet points (like this one)
- album cover images
- bold sub headlines

Draw attention to the things you want people to read, know about, and click on (like the music "Play" button or ezine subscription form).

#21

Spell Out Your "Call to Action"

On each page of your artist web site, you should have a goal – something you want a visitor to DO while on that page. It might be listen to a song, subscribe to your ezine, come to a live show, purchase a CD, etc. Whatever it is, make that clear and include a call to action – clear instructions to do that thing now!

#22

Watch Someone Surf Your Web Site

Corporate types call this "usability testing." You can call it whatever you want, but you'll learn a lot by simply watching different people go to your web site for the first time, even if they are just friends and family members. Don't interrupt or make suggestions. Just observe. Then ask and answer questions. This exercise will prove invaluable when it comes to making your web site better and more "user friendly."

#23

Browse, Rate, Borrow and Tweak

Another thing you can do is visit lots of other artists' web sites and simply note what you like and dislike about them. Try to incorporate your favorite features and keep a watchful eye on the negative design aspects that may have accidentally slipped into your own web site. Then correct them as soon as possible!

#24

Let People Know What Kind of Music You Play

One of the biggest web site marketing mistakes I see involves bands or record labels that list a name with a busy design ... and then make no mention of what kind of music they play or why people should care. Always make a reference to the type of music you perform. In fact, I recommend you include a descriptive phrase (such as "Soft sounds to center your mind, body and soul" or "Old-school funk for people who like to dance," or whatever applies to you) somewhere near the top of *every page* on your web site.

#25

Assume Nothing – Learn to See With Fresh Eyes

This is such an important thing to keep in mind. Always view your web site (and all of your online marketing efforts, for that matter) through the eyes of someone discovering you for the first time.

Don't ever assume that a person visiting your web site already knows who you are, what type of music you play, and why that's such a great thing. Try to imagine what someone stumbling upon your site will think as they set their eyes upon it for the first time.

Ask Yourself These Questions

- Is the web page clear and easy to understand?

- Do you make it obvious what your musical style and genre are?

- Do you give people a reason to click deeper into your web site to learn more?

- If someone arrives at your site on a page other than the home page, will they still know immediately what it's all about?

It seems so obvious, but you'd be surprised by the vast number of vague and mysterious music web sites scattered about the Internet. They feature a large photo of the artist, his or her name, and cryptic verbiage such as, "A musical masterpiece" or "Winner of four songwriting awards" or, my favorite, "Music that defies definition!"

Sadly, few people will ever truly embrace this artist's music, because the web site doesn't provide a clue as to what it is and how it benefits the visitor. Make certain *your* web site communicates clearly.

#26

Create Web Page Navigation That Is Simple and Obvious

How easy is it to get around your web site? If you want fans and music business people to truly dig into your site, you must make it easy for them to move from page to page. Your "navigation bar," which usually sits along the top or side of *every* page, lists the main sections of your site.

Keep this list of internal links short. Limit it to the basics: Bio, Shows, Music, Photos, Reviews, Order, Links, Contact. Make sure the navigation section appears in the exact same spot on every page. It's also a good idea to repeat these section links in a smaller navigation area at the bottom of every page. If your site is lacking in clear, consistent navigation, fix this right away!

#27

Make Sure Your Web Site Is Easily Viewed on Smartphones and Tablets

Warning: Please don't gloss over this tip. If you do, you could make your web site inaccessible to the majority of people who try to visit it. So pay close attention ...

There's a huge trend taking place that is outgrowing even the most liberal predictions by experts in recent years. I'm talking about the widespread use of smartphones and tablet computers. According to Eric Schmidt, Google's CEO, mobile use is growing much quicker than anyone expected. "It's happening faster than all of our predictions," he said during a recent keynote speech.

Along with that trend, of course, the use of desktop PCs is shrinking. A Morgan Stanley report found that the amount of time people spend on PCs dropped 20% between 2008 and 2010. The use of mobile phones to access the Internet is also growing in continents such as South America and Asia. So ...

This is a reality you need to brace for now!

If your artist or music company web site was designed to look cool on a desktop computer, it very well may not be so cool when viewed on a smartphone. Be sure to look at your web site on a variety of mobile devices: iPhone, Android, Blackberry, etc. The same thing applies to the iPad and other tablet computers, which are also growing in popularity.

Make certain your site loads quickly in various mobile browsers. Do away with Flash and heavy graphic elements. Make it easy for people to hear and purchase your music using whatever Internet connection device they choose to use!

Bottom line: a simple design makes for easy access.

#28
Give Away Some of Your Music for Free

Too many musicians are stingy with their music. They hoard their song files and guard them from the evil downloading freeloaders. Sure, you can protect your songs to a reasonable extent. But as an indie artist, your goal is to share your music and get it into the ears of as many people as possible. That means potential fans must be able to *hear* your music and have the ability to share it with their friends.

My advice: Select the two or three best songs from each album you release and make them available for download to whoever wants them. Encourage widespread sharing of these files. You want people playing them at home, transferring them to their iPods, burning them to CDs, and spreading the buzz. Then, if these new fans want more of the great music you create, they can purchase your entire album (or song collection download).

The fans who discover you via free downloads may someday financially support you in many other ways: live show admission fees, T-shirt and merchandise sales, hiring you for private parties, and more. So give away at least some of your music with no strings attached. This goodwill could easily come back to you in surprising ways.

#29
Add Interactivity to Your Web Site

One way to get people involved with you and your music is to give them something to do while they're at your web site. That's why you should add some kind of interactive element, such as a poll, guest book, message forum, e-cards, etc.

Here are some sites that provide interactive tools for free:

Bravenet
www.bravenet.com

Mister Poll
www.misterpoll.com

Sparklit
www.sparklit.com

Survey Monkey
www.surveymonkey.com

Widgetbox
www.widgetbox.com

The fans who discover you via free downloads may someday financially support you in many other ways: live show admission fees, T-shirt and merchandise sales, hiring you for private parties, and more. So give away at least some of your music with no strings attached. This goodwill could easily come back to you in surprising ways.

#29
Add Interactivity to Your Web Site

One way to get people involved with you and your music is to give them something to do while they're at your web site. That's why you should add some kind of interactive element, such as a poll, guest book, message forum, e-cards, etc.

Here are some sites that provide interactive tools for free:

Bravenet
www.bravenet.com

Mister Poll
www.misterpoll.com

Sparklit
www.sparklit.com

Survey Monkey
www.surveymonkey.com

Widgetbox
www.widgetbox.com

Now let's consider a rewrite of the previous example ...

Good Use of Title Tags

```
<title>Snuggle Doodle - Music for children,
toddlers and kids of all ages</title>
```

This tag is much more effective. It is based on the educated assumption that potential buyers are searching online using phrases such as "children's music," "music for kids," and "music for children." Notice how all of those words appear in the Title tag above. (Note: Please don't search for Snuggle Doodle; I made it up.)

Tip: Each page on your site should have a different Title tag based on the content of that page. For instance, if the creator of Snuggle Doodle also had a page of free music downloads, the Title tag for that page might read:

```
<title>Free music for kids, children's music
downloads</title>
```

See how this works? It's all about being as clear, specific and descriptive as possible.

#31

Place an Ezine Subscription Link on Every Page of Your Web Site

Publishing a fan ezine is one thing. Having a lot of fan subscribers is another. Your goal is to get as many people as possible to subscribe. This growing list of people who are interested in your music holds the key to your success. So the more subscribers you have, the merrier!

One way to encourage sign-ups is to put an ezine subscription link in a prominent spot on every page of your web site. Don't bury this important call to action. Make it part of the simple navigation bar (discussed in Tip #26) that appears on every page of your web site.

Really do this. Take a close look at your web site right now. Is an ezine subscription option blatantly obvious? If not, figure out a way to make it stand out, and change the page design accordingly.

#32
Show Your Personality

As you've hopefully figured out by now, I believe your web site and fan email newsletter exist to serve a purpose far beyond making gig announcements and music sales pitches. Your primary mission with these promotion vehicles is to start and nurture relationships with a growing number of fans. One of the ways fans come to know and love you is by getting to know who you are as a human being. They want to know the person or people behind the music and what makes them tick.

Therefore, reveal yourself and your personality on the Web and via email. Share stories and anecdotes that tap into the emotions and vibe of your songs. For example, here are three artists who do a good job of showing their personalities on their web sites and ezines:

Christine Kane
www.christinekane.com/site/bio/

Groovy Judy
www.groovyjudy.com

Mike Doughty
www.mkdo.co

#33

Make Sure Your Web Pages Are Search Engine Friendly

To improve your chances of ranking well in search engine results, the words that appear throughout a web page should compliment the words that appear in that page's Title, Meta Description, and Meta Keywords tags.

These two online tools will help you analyze your pages for free:

Keyword Density Analyzer
tools.seobook.com/general/keyword-density

Meta Tag Analyzer
www.submitexpress.com/analyzer

Not sure what all this talk about meta tags and keyword density is about? It's a topic beyond the scope of this book, but it is important stuff to know. So check out these three online resources for further guidance:

META Tag Guide
www.submitcorner.com/Guide/Meta

Meta tags - what, where, when, why?
www.philb.com/metatag.htm

Keyword Density
www.seochat.com/seo-tools/keyword-density

#34

Submit Your Site to Search Engines and Directories

Once you're confident that your site is ready for the world to see, you can submit it to various search engines and directories. Usually, search spiders (programs that "crawl" the web to record what is located where) will eventually find their way to your site and index it anyway. But you may be able to speed things along by submitting them yourself.

Your best bet is to go to each search engine or directory and submit individually. Here are the pages where you can do that at some of the biggest sites:

Google
www.google.com/addurl

Bing
www.bing.com/docs/submit.aspx

Yahoo
siteexplorer.search.yahoo.com/submit

Open Directory
www.dmoz.org/add.html

MusicMoz
www.musicmoz.org/add.html

Find more music directories at www.dmoz.org/Arts/Music/Directories

#35

Accept Payments From Your Own Web Site

You may already know that your fans can order your albums and singles securely online when you get set up with CD Baby or Amazon. But what if you want to take orders right from your own site? And what if you want to sell T-shirts, caps, and other merchandise? CD Baby and Amazon can't help you there. Here are six payment processing services to consider using:

PayPal.com
www.paypal.com

Google Checkout
checkout.google.com

Amazon Payments
payments.amazon.com

2CheckOut.com
www.2checkout.com

ClickBank.com (digital products only)
www.clickbank.com

CCnow.com
www.ccnow.com

Look over fees and policies carefully. Most have a per-transaction fee plus a percentage of each sale. But look them all over and see what will work best for you.

#36

Make Compelling Offers and Ask for the Sale

Some people make a purchase right away when something interests them. Some rarely make a purchase. And a lot of people teeter on the fence, not sure which direction to go. For these folks in the middle, you need to create incentives – reasons for them to hit the Buy button now.

Here are some compelling ways to nudge them into making a purchase:

- **Limited-time discounts**: Get a 20% discount if you purchase by this Friday.
- **Limited-quantity offers**: The first 25 people who respond get an autographed copy.
- **Upsell with a special offer**: Buy one, get one free. Or buy our new album, get our previous release at half off.
- **Bundling**: Purchase a CD, T-shirt and cap at the same time, save 50%.
- **Charity benefit**: 20% of all music sales proceeds tonight go to the local Wildlife Refuge.

#37

Write Benefit-Rich "YOU" Descriptions

The Internet can be a cold, mechanical place. There's nothing inherently warm and fuzzy about a computer or mobile phone screen. Your job as a caring, fan-building, guerrilla music marketer is to make an online interaction with you as warm and inviting as possible. When writing about yourself, your gigs, and your for-sale items, do everything you can to make your words come to life as a one-on-one conversation.

Don't be sterile. Don't write "Listeners will enjoy the energetic arrangements and lush harmonies …" Barf. Who are these listeners you're writing about? They're the people sitting in front of a screen many miles away using up their precious time to read about you. Speak directly to them. Make it count. Make it interesting.

Write something along the lines of, "If you like to shake your butt on the dance floor, you'll love this album. Imagine the groovin' atmosphere you'll create at your next party with our music. Your friends will love you. Strangers will be in awe. You might even get lucky …"

See the difference? Speak directly to your fans, like each one was sitting face to face across the table from you. Help them conjure up how they'll enjoy and benefit from your music. Help them mentally picture how they'll use your music. Doing so will make their decision to hit the Subscribe or Buy button a lot easier.

#38

Make Digital Images Available on Your Web Site

If you actively pursue publicity, you've no doubt been asked to supply an artist photo or image of your album cover art. These days, publications (both print and Web-based) like to deal with digital images.

You will make a lot of editors happy by making digital images available for download from your web site. And make them available in both high-resolution (300 dpi for print publications) and low-resolution (72 dpi for the Web) versions. These links don't have to be part of your public site. Just have them ready when an editor asks.

Lesson: Make it easy for the media to cover you!

#39

Hold Online Contests and Giveaways

People like to win things. And they don't mind having to perform some minor task to earn the prize. In addition, many people are enticed by friendly competitions. Make the most of this human response by holding contests and giving away free stuff from your web site.

Perhaps you can award a free CD or album download to one new ezine subscriber every month. Or ask your fans to help you name a new song or album title. The winning entry gets five free copies of the CD. Use your imagination and find fun ways to get people involved and excited about interacting with you online.

#40

Start a Genre-Specific Music Site

Having a web site that promotes your band and sells your music is great. You need to do that. But some smart musicians have benefited greatly from taking things a step further. Remember, your goal is to reach people online who are interested in your style of music. What better way to do that than to start a web site that acts as a resource on your entire musical genre — not just you as a single artist or band.

For instance, solo piano artist David Nevue (www.davidnevue.com) started **Whisperings: Solo Piano Radio** (www.solopianoradio.com), a site that features links and reviews of dozens of complimentary artists — with occasional mentions of his own live shows and albums.

Likewise, Irish folk musician Marc Gunn (www.marcgunn.com) also runs **Celtic MP3s Music Magazine** (www.celticmp3s.com), a site that attracts fans of ... you guessed it, Celtic music, while also sending web traffic to his personal site.

Great idea. If you have a little extra time to spend on this idea, it could do wonders for your popularity!

(By the way, David Nevue is also the author of a great book called **How to Promote Your Music Successfully on the Internet**. Learn more about it at http://goo.gl/V3Gfc.)

#41

Make a Global Impact With Google Translation

Music is a universal language. People throughout the world love songs sung in English, while music fans of all ethnicities often enjoy music from other cultures. The only problem is, music consumers generally search for things using their native language. Which means a lot of people around the world may never find you.

Wouldn't it be great if some of your web pages were available in multiple languages? In the past, you'd have to invest in a translator to do that. But these days, you can use Google's little-known free translation service at translate.google.com.

Go there now and enter the URL of a page on your site. Select the original language and the language you want it translated into. Click "Translate" and watch your page instantly transform. Pretty amazing.

However, your best bet may be to add Google's free web site translator feature to your web pages. That way, anyone who visits your site can convert it to the language of their choice. Give it a try. Details at translate.google.com/translate_tools.

Just note that this free and automated translation function isn't perfect. It would be best to have someone very familiar with the other language to edit the page to avoid any awkward or unintended meanings.

Ready to start drawing people to this wonderful music web site you've just built? That's what we cover in Section Three.

Promoting Your Music Across the Internet

Now that you have a firm grasp of marketing principles and a solid music web site hub, it's time to reach out and start connecting with your ideal fans. Use the tactics in this section to create awareness and lure people into your musical world.

#42

Plug Into Genre Filters

This will come as no surprise to you, but I'll state the obvious anyway: The Internet is a crowded and noisy place. There are so many people, so many sites to sift through, so many information sources, so many applications and new widgets, so many choices ... it's staggering.

If you feel that way, just think about your potential fans. They feel overwhelmed too. The good news is, people don't have to wade through everything available online to find what they want. These days, there are a growing number of "filters" that help consumers quickly get the exact information they need.

What's a filter?

The most prominent and obvious example of a filter is the mega search site Google.com. It's often the first place people go to hunt down information they are looking for.

Facts: According to StatOwl.com, Google accounts for 78% of all search engine usage. Yahoo.com and Microsoft's Bing.com each have about 9% of the search market. Ask.com and AOL.com each have less than 2%.

But search sites aren't the only filters people use to seek out and discover new music online. Other filters include:

- Personal recommendations from friends (the most potent filter of all)
- Customer reviews and ratings
- Trusted bloggers and podcasters
- Coverage in traditional and online media
- Bestseller lists
- Genre-specific web sites

This is just a short list of filter examples, but hopefully it will help to cement another important principle into your ever-expanding guerrilla marketing mind ...

Key insight: When promoting yourself and your music online, you must tap into the filters that *your ideal fans* are using to find music online!

#43
Create a Trail of "Link Bait"

Hopefully, pieces of the online music promotion puzzle are starting to come together for you and create a clear picture. You now understand the role of your artist web site and realize the value of tapping into genre filters.

There's one more concept I want to cover before we get into the mechanics of spreading your message online. I'm talking about "link bait." It's a pretty simple concept, but I'm constantly surprised by how often it eludes even the smartest musicians and music promoters.

As the Internet expands, people have become increasingly mesmerized by Web 2.0 technologies, multimedia, and a growing number of interactive features. That's great, but it has caused people to lose sight of a key factor.

Important: When it comes to finding things online, the Internet is still a text-based, word-driven medium. When people go to Google, they type in words and phrases related to what they're looking for.

Likewise, when they are scanning blogs and information sites, they are attracted to headlines and descriptions that contain words directly related to their interests.

Don't underestimate the power of this reality. So many people pay lip service to this idea and say, "Oh yeah, I get it." But when you examine their music promotion efforts, they miss the target.

Don't make this same mistake!

From now on, whenever you post new audio files, video clips, photos, blog posts, web pages, and more ... fill them with "link bait." Load them up, in a natural and sensible way, with the words and phrases of interest to your specific type of fan.

For example, if you perform nerdcore (a niche form of hip-hop for ... you guessed it, nerds) you should include the word "nerdcore" prominently in the titles and descriptions of the media you post online. Also, make references to the most prominent acts in your genre (in the case of nerdcore, that would be MC Frontalot, High-C, MC Lars, Ytcracker, and others).

In short, leave a trail of word bait that will attract your ideal type of music fan!

#44

Use Popular, Similar Artists to Help Define You

Music fans, especially people who are learning about you for the first time, need to categorize your music in their brains. Not to pigeonhole you, but to help them store details about you in their memory. One important way people accomplish this is by comparing you to other artists they already enjoy. You can help this process along by dropping a few names of your own.

David Nevue (www.davidnevue.com), whom I mentioned earlier, used to use this text near the top of his home page: "If you're into Yanni, George Winston or Jim Brickman's piano music, you'll love this ..."

Note how David squeezed in the names of three prominent artists in his genre, and the phrase "piano music," into one short sentence. That's smart marketing! So ... mention other similar artists, and help new fans make the mental connection quicker.

#45

Add Extra Words to Your Peer-to-Peer Song Listings

Do you make your original songs available through file-sharing (P2P) sites such as BitTorrent or Gnutella? That might be a good idea if you want to get your music to lots of people who might be willing to listen.

Hot tip: Some acts have gotten more out of these peer-to-peer networks by adding a similar popular act's name to their artist name when logging songs. For instance, "Amy Smith (like Jewel)" will come up in P2P searches for Jewel. That will increase the odds of Amy's music reaching more potential fans than "Amy Smith" alone.

For a long list of digital file-sharing applications, visit
en.wikipedia.org/wiki/Comparison_of_file_sharing_applications

#46

Sell Your Recordings at CD Baby

You probably already know about and do this, but just in case … No
discussion of online music promotion would be complete without
talking about CD Baby (www.cdbaby.com). It's the #1 indie music sales
site in the world. Since 1998, the site has sold several million physical
CDs online to customers and paid more than $157 million directly to
artists. If you have a CD for sale, you need to make it available there.

In addition, the service allows artists to sell downloads from the CD
Baby site as well as on iTunes, Amazon MP3 and others. It can also
hook you up to take credit card orders at live gigs, sell or give away
download cards, and get plugged into distribution to thousands of
music retail stores.

CD Baby founder Derek Sivers sold the company in 2008 to Disc
Makers, which has made a lot of improvements to what was already a
great service for indie artists. For an overview of what CD Baby
currently offers, visit members.cdbaby.com.

#47

Sell Your Digital Downloads Using Tunecore

With physical CD sales continuing to decline and music download sales
on the rise, everyone wants to get their music on iTunes, Napster,
Emusic, Rhapsody, and other digital music sales sites. The good news
is, it's never been easier for independent artists to do just that. One
way is to go through CD Baby, covered in the previous tip. Another

prominent site that offers this service is Tunecore (www.tunecore.com).

While CD Baby charges few upfront costs to get your music on iTunes and the others, they do take an ongoing percentage as their fee (currently 9% of the net sales). Tunecore uses a different model: They charge a set fee per song, per album and per store you want it sold in, and then you keep all the revenue after that.

With both sites you can now register a single song if you want – a great way to go if you have a hot track you want to promote but no full album to go with it.

Visit this page for more details on Tunecore: www.tunecore.com/index/about.

Note: You can't use both CD Baby and Tunecore for digital distribution. You must choose one service or the other.

#48

Submit Your Music News to These Sites for Free

Many web sites are hungry for fresh music news, and some are eager to share your news releases and announcements with the world online. Visit the following links and submit away!

Music Industry News Network
www.mi2n.com/input.php3

Pressbox
www.pressbox.co.uk

Muse's Muse
www.musesmuse.com/pressreleases

PR Log
www.prlog.org

Indie-Music.com
www.indie-music.com/contact.php

Great Music Sites
www.greatmusicsites.com/newssubmission.htm

PR.com
www.pr.com/promote-your-business

#49

Promote Your Live Shows on These Sites for Free

This is where the real world meets the virtual world. Yes, you can and should use the Internet to promote your live, in-the-flesh gigs. The reverse is also true: You should use your live performances to drive traffic to your web site.

Visit the appropriate sites below to promote your live events for free online:

Upcoming
upcoming.yahoo.com

JamBase
www.jambase.com

Musi-Cal
www.musi-cal.com

Mojam
mojam.wolfgangsvault.com/contribute

Facebook events
www.facebook.com/?sk=events

Craigslist
www.craigslist.org

I'll cover more on Facebook and Craigslist in Section Four.

#50

Use Artist Data to Automate Your Gig Listings and More

This is a site, now owned by SonicBids, that many musicians rave about. Go to www.artistdata.com and sign up for a free account. This will allow you to automatically post your live show listings, blog feeds, and status updates across multiple sites such as MySpace, Facebook, and Twitter. Note: The site may offer a premium paid version bundled with SonicBids at some point.

It's a potentially powerful platform that could save you from having to log in to several sites and accounts to repost the same information. Artist Data also offers a couple of paid levels that provide extra features. Worth checking out!

#51

Get Exposure on MP3 Blogs and Music Review Sites

Music reviews used to be one of the primary ways that music publicists got exposure for new album releases. Not so much anymore, in my opinion. Don't get me wrong, you should still pursue music reviews. But these days, they should be just one small part of your overall marketing strategy.

In years past, everyone wanted to get their album or live show reviewed in the major media – from *Billboard* and *Rolling Stone* to *SPIN* and the local alternative weekly. There was a lot of competition, which lead to limited opportunities for independent artists and promoters.

Good news: Today, the definition of "media exposure" has greatly expanded. There are now thousands (perhaps millions) of web sites and blogs that review and feature music. That can be both a blessing and a curse. But with some smart searching, you should be able to uncover some ideal sites to target for reviews and exposure.

When it comes to online music review sites, **Pitchfork** (www.pitchfork.com) is one of the most sought after. Some publications have cited Pitchfork as having played a role in "breaking" artists such as Arcade Fire, Broken Social Scene, Clap Your Hands Say Yeah, and Modest Mouse.

Other prominent music sites include **Brooklyn Vegan** (www.brooklynvegan.com), **Music Critic** (www.music-critic.com) and **Spinner** (www.spinner.com).

But there are also countless lesser-known sites where you can get exposure – including MP3 blogs that feature either streaming or downloadable music files (often with the permission and encouragement of the artists who created them).

Here are two great places to search for targeted music blogs:

Google Blog Search
blogsearch.google.com

Captain Crawl
www.captaincrawl.com

Bonus resource: One awesome place to find links to prominent music blogs that tend to be "indie friendly" is the **Hype Machine** (www.hypem.com). This site aggregates the feeds of hundreds of music blogs – which makes it a perfect site for music promotion research.

#52

Tap Into Music Alley (Formerly the Podsafe Music Network)

This is the site where podcasters go to find music that has been deemed "podsafe." That means the copyright holders of the music available on Music Alley give permission to podcasters to play their songs. Many indie acts have received a lot of online exposure as a result of having an account there. Learn more at www.musicalley.com.

#53

Discover Radio Airplay Opportunities

Find out everything you need to know about radio stations across town, across the country, or around the world. Use these directories to uncover radio gold:

Radio-Locator
www.radio-locator.com

Gebbie Press
www.gebbieinc.com/radintro.htm

Radio Station Directory – UK
www.mediauk.com/radio

#54

Research Public Radio Stations

As you may know, public and community radio stations are often easier to get airplay on than commercial stations. Use these sites to find out where the best public radio stations and programs are.

Public Radio Fan
www.publicradiofan.com

List of NPR stations
www.npr.org/stations

Open Directory - Public Radio
www.dmoz.org/Arts/Radio/Formats/Public_Radio

#55

Find Internet Radio Stations

There's been an explosion of streaming online radio stations in recent years. Some are the online versions of traditional broadcast stations; many others are independent stations run by hardcore music fans. Use these directories to find stations that support your style, and contact them for possible online airplay.

SHOUTcast
www.shoutcast.com

Radio Free World
www.radiofreeworld.com

Live365
www.live365.com

Radio Tower
www.radiotower.com

Stream Finder
www.streamfinder.com

#56

Uncover Newspapers and Magazines

Research ain't what it used to be. No reference librarian is required to hunt down thousands of newspapers and magazines across the globe. Use these sites to search for writers, reviewers and editors who may cover you.

RefDesk - Newspapers
www.refdesk.com/paper.html

NewsLink
www.newslink.org/news.html

AllYouCanRead.com – Magazines
www.allyoucanread.com

Daily Earth
www.dailyearth.com

International Newspaper Directory
www.nettizen.com/newspaper

Internet Public Library
www.ipl.org/div/news

#57

Start Relationships With 5 to 10 Regional Media People

Media people are your friends – or they can be, *if* you develop relationships with them. Think about your local media outlets and select a handful of writers, editors, producers, show hosts, etc., who you feel would be the most likely to give you exposure at some point. Don't make this a long list. Five to 10 local media people is plenty to start. Create a file and put their names and contact info into it.

First, send an email to introduce yourself. Don't be pushy at this point. Just get acquainted. Then every month or so, send an update with some new details on your progress. After a while, try to reach them by phone too. These relationships will bear fruit over the coming months and years.

#58

Use the Personal PR Approach

One big change in publicity that has taken place over the past decade is that most editors, producers and writers now prefer to get news releases (and even entire press kits) by email or in some digital form online. Not only does this trend save trees, but it makes it easier for you to reach a lot of media people in a faster and more efficient way. So by all means, take your properly formatted press releases and send them as text within the body of an email. (Only send an attached file when someone knows you or has requested it.)

However, don't end your PR efforts there. One of the most effective, time-tested ways to get media coverage is to communicate one on one with media people using personal messages. Instead of sending Joe Scribe in Dallas the same generic release that Jane Journalist in

Denver gets, send Joe a more conversational personal note: "Joe, Here's a story idea for your March issue ..."

Then briefly explain why your story will be good for his publication in his city. Make sure it reads like an articulate note to a friend or business associate, not just an impersonal announcement. If you start doing this, I bet you'll see an immediate increase in the media relationships you build.

Personal communication is always better than generic. Always.

#59
Plug Your Web Site During Media Interviews

Your artist web site shouldn't operate in a vacuum. Ideally, it should feed your real-world, offline activities. And what you do offline should cross-promote your online presence. Therefore, when you do land a traditional print or broadcast interview, be sure to make the most of the opportunity and send people to your web site.

But ... you have to be strategic about it. Anyone can say, "If you want to find out more about the band, visit our web site at ..." Yawn.

Instead, create a valuable resource that's easy to describe on the air or during an interview, and make it available from your web site. A free download of one of your songs probably won't cut it. Give it more widespread appeal and have it tie in directly with your musical identity.

Example: "I'd like to offer your listeners a free report called *The Top 10 Jazz CDs of All Time*. You can download it right from our web site at ..." Or "Your viewers can help themselves to a free report called *Ten Ways to Use Music to Relax and De-Stress Your Life*. It's available at ..."

See how valuable this would be in attracting new fans to your web site?

#60

Don't Forget Your Local Music Scene Web Sites

This should be obvious, but just in case ... Make sure you have a list of web sites that cover your local music scene. A lot of these have popped up over the years, run by hard-core fans or wannabe journalists. These local sites can be easy places to get exposure. Some review locally produced albums and live shows, others post gig schedules, and some do full-blown interviews and feature stories.

Tip: Doing a Google search for "music (your city name)" should help uncover a lot of these sites in your area.

#61

Follow Up With Everyone

Once is not enough. Especially when it comes to email messages you send to media people, potential cross-promotion partners, and music industry people of all kinds.

The thing is, most music promoters don't connect a second or third time with people they try to reach. To these self-defeating marketers, a lack of response must mean a lack of interest – that the artist or proposed idea isn't worthy. But that isn't always the case.

People are busy. They may be interested in your proposal but get sidetracked and forget about you. Not to worry. A friendly reminder note can be just the thing to reawaken their intentions to get back to you. Or it can be the trigger that inspires them to more seriously consider your idea and make a decision on it.

The difference between success and failure can often be measured in mere inches. Following up is just one way you can set yourself apart and make people wonder how you got so lucky to enjoy all the exposure that seems to naturally come your way.

#62

Get on Bestseller, Most Popular and Most Downloaded Lists

True music fans hate to miss out on the latest craze within their preferred genre. One of the ways fans discover what's hot is by looking over the growing number of popularity lists on various music web sites. These lists come in all shapes and sizes: Top Sellers, Most Listened To, Most Popular Downloads, etc. The higher your ranking on these lists, the more attention you draw to yourself.

So how can you get visibility on these lists? Well, writing and recording a fantastic song and getting it out there is the first step. An audience will find a killer song through word of mouth alone. But you can help things along by asking your fans and friends to visit, vote, download, listen or whatever it takes to help you rank higher on these lists.

Suggestion: Pick one such list on one site in a category where you feel pretty confident you can make an impact. Ask the people on your mailing list to visit that site and take the required action on the same day or during the same week. This concentrated effort may be all it takes to get you to move higher on the list, where other fans who don't know about you yet will discover you.

#63

Find New Connections With Advanced Google Searches

One of the funniest web sites I've seen lately is www.LetMeGoogleThatForYou.com. Its purpose: "This is for all those people who find it more convenient to bother you with their question rather than Google it for themselves."

I know the feeling. I've lost count of the number of times someone has asked me a question like, "What's the best way to learn HTML?" When I ask, "Have you tried searching Google for HTML how-to sites?" ... more often than not, the reply is, "Well, um ... no."

So, just in case this has escaped you, there's a world of information at your fingertips, if you only go to a search site like Google and seek it out.

But that's just a starting point. Doing a quick search for something is one thing. But knowing a few advanced tricks can help you discover more and richer finds on the Internet. Here are my top four advanced searching techniques:

Use Variations of Keyword Phrases

Let's say you want to compile a list of sites that might review your new album of French folk songs. Of course, you can go to Google and enter "French folk songs" into the search field.

Then, one by one, you visit the web pages that come up in the search results. You would then bookmark or in some way compile a list of the most promising music sites. Job well done, right?

Not so fast!

Go back and also search for variations and alternate phrases related to French folk songs, such as: French folk music, folk songs from France, traditional French music, classic French songs, etc. Each phrase will bring a different set of search results. So don't stop after the first or second search.

Use Quotation Marks

Google has some pretty cool advanced features. One of the simplest involves the use of quotation marks. Let me explain: In a normal search, such as the previous French folk songs example, Google returns pages that display the words "French" and "folk" and "songs" anywhere on the page. That's fine, but you will have many sites turn up that have nothing to do with music from Europe.

When you put quotation marks around a phrase in the search field, Google will give you only pages that use those words together in that exact order. Therefore, the results are more likely to be accurate matches for what you're looking for. If you don't do this already, start using quotation marks to fine-tune your searches.

Use the "Related" Search Function

To the right of the normal Google search box you'll see a small link that says "Advanced Search." If you've never clicked it, please do, because there you'll find a lot of useful search options. And once on that page, be sure to click "Date, usage rights, numeric range, and more" for two of my favorite Google search tricks.

Under "Page-specific tools," you'll find a box with the description "Find pages similar to the page." How do you use this feature? Let's say you just discovered www.AlohaMagazine.com, and it's the ideal type of site to promote your new Hawaiian slack key guitar album. If you could just find more web sites similar to that one, you'd be in hula heaven.

You see where I'm going with this. Just enter www.AlohaMagazine.com into that "similar to" field and you'll find other sites like it.

Quick tip: There's a faster way to access this Google feature. Just enter the word "related," a colon, and then the web address into the regular search box, as in "related:www.AlohaMagazine.com" – no need to use the quotes; I just did that to set them apart.

Use the "Link" Search Function

Finally, one of my favorite advanced Google search techniques: The "Find pages that link to the page" option, which will reveal pages that link to any page or site you enter. How is this one helpful?

If you write songs that would appeal to fans of Mary Chapin Carpenter, you can quickly hunt down sites that link to Carpenter's by entering "link:www.marychapincarpenter.com" into the regular search box (again, without the quotes). This trick alone can uncover online music exposure gold.

The next time you wonder where you should focus your Internet marketing efforts, use these advanced search features to find exactly the right web sites for you and your music.

Bonus tip: Search using a word related to your style of music combined with the phrase "submit your music" or "submit your music news" or "send us your CD."

#64

Start Relationships With 5 to 10 Complimentary Artists

In the same way I recommend you establish relationships with five to 10 regional media people, I encourage you to also do that with other similar artists. It would be helpful if the artists you target have good-sized followings and are not paranoid about sharing their audiences and resources with you.

Key: That's the whole idea here – to work together to help each other succeed.

Here are just a few ways you can make the most of these artist relationships:

- Swap promotional plugs in each other's fan ezines and on Facebook, Twitter, etc.
- Trade links on each other's web sites.
- Review and recommend each other's albums online.
- Share media lists and industry connections.
- Share promotion tips and advice on what works and what doesn't.
- Open for each other in your respective hometowns.

#65
Write and Distribute Articles

This could be one of the most overlooked opportunities to promote your music on the Internet. Usually, when musicians think of getting exposure on music web sites, they think of getting a review of their new album or a feature story written about them. That's fine. But if you have a decent command of the language and can string a few sentences together, you should also consider *writing* articles for these same music sites.

You can write and submit album reviews, band interviews, commentaries, and more. You won't get paid for most of these submissions, but the payoff is that these sites will allow you to include a blurb at the end of each article that details who you are, what type of music you play, and how readers can find out more about you.

Here are some music sites that will consider your article submissions:

MusicDish e-Journal
www.musicdish.com

The Muse's Muse
www.musesmuse.com

Indie-Music
www.indie-music.com

Hypebot
www.hypebot.com

You could also open a free account at one of these general "article repository" sites and start posting your own prose for extra online exposure:

#66

Start a Live 365 Station

Do you ever get sick of the stations and shows available on your radio dial? Of course you do. Have you ever thought, "If I could afford it, I'd start my own station and play the music I love – the cool stuff that rarely gets played." Well, now you can. In fact, there are many ways to do that these days. One good way is by using www.Live365.com, an online service that allows you to program and broadcast your own streaming radio station for as little as $10 a month.

The obvious thing you should do with your station's play list is load it with lots of your own songs. But you'll make it more valuable for fans if you also include some great tracks from other indie and well-known artists in your genre. An awesome, highly focused show may get you exposure on blogs and music sites that cover your genre, not to mention through the other acts that you feature on your show. And all the people who give it a listen will be treated to … you guessed it, *your music!*

#67

Join Amazon.com's Advantage Program

It may not seem to be the music haven that iTunes and CD Baby are, but Amazon gets so much traffic, it shouldn't be ignored. Millions of people visit the site every day, and many go looking for new music, especially at the Amazon MP3 store. So you really should have your music on Amazon.

There are a number of ways to make your music available for sale directly from Amazon. If you use a distributor, they may handle that for you. But you can make the arrangements yourself by joining Amazon's Advantage program (details at advantage.amazon.com).

There's a $29.95 annual program fee (per account, not per album title), and you must be willing to part with 55% of your album's retail price. That's right, you'll end up with 45% of the suggested retail price you set.

Reality check: Many musicians cry foul over the percentage split, but come on! You'd give a traditional distributor a big chunk of the retail price anyway. Amazon serves a similar function, and it reaches millions of online music buyers. So just bite the bullet and make your music available on the site.

Note that when you join the Advantage program, you must ship CDs to Amazon promptly in the amounts they order, which will ramp up or down as each album's sales figures warrant. It's more hands-on than the CreateSpace option I'll cover in a moment, but it's a viable way you should be aware of. You can also make your songs available for sale in the Amazon MP3 store with an Advantage program account.

#68

Get Sound Clips on Your Amazon Sales Page

Obviously, you want people to be able to sample streaming clips of your songs while on your Amazon sales page. Once you're part of Amazon's Advantage program, be sure to sign in to your account and look for instructions on how to submit your music sound clips.

#69

Submit Your CD Cover Art

According to the Amazon site, "Showing a picture of a CD's cover on its Amazon.com page is an item's most influential selling point. We'll add the cover image to your item's detail page for free." Again, sign in to your Advantage account and look for the "Upload Cover Art" link.

#70

Consider Amazon's CreateSpace Service

Amazon also runs a company called CreateSpace that produces print-on-demand CDs, DVDs and books for independent artists, record labels, authors, and more. If you're looking for a more "hands off" method of getting your music on Amazon, CreateSpace may be an ideal solution.

According to the site: "Distribute your music on Amazon.com and other sales channels as an audio CD or MP3 download. Set the list price for your audio CDs and choose from a selection of royalty plans for your MP3 downloads. Use our online tools to set up your titles –

they're free! Since copies of your titles are manufactured as customers order, you'll never worry about inventory and set-up fees."

Visit www.createspace.com to learn more.

#71

Create Your Amazon Artist Central Account

For a few years now, Amazon has given authors the ability to create a special author profile page on the site. It's great to see this feature finally available to musicians too.

Here's Amazon's description: "Artist Central enables musicians, record labels and managers to upload official content to www.amazon.com artist stores. You can upload MP3s for free streaming, official photos, videos, a biography, a Twitter feed, and a page banner."

Visit artistcentral.amazon.com to sign up.

#72

Ask Your Fans to Post Reviews

Amazon was one of the first sites to make significant use of user-generated reviews. And what a valuable asset they've become. Try walking into Best Buy or Walmart sometime and asking a clerk, "Can you tell me what the last 10 people who bought this CD thought of it?" They'd think you were crazy.

But on Amazon, you can find out immediately how other people rated the album you are considering buying. It's a major factor that influences a lot of purchase decisions on the site.

So, how can you make good use of reviews?

Do this: Encourage your most supportive fans to post positive reviews on your album's Amazon sales page. I believe that a person must purchase at least one item from Amazon to be able to write reviews, so not everyone will be able to randomly post their glowing testimonials. But I'm sure many of your fans have bought something from the site and have accounts there already.

This is a no-brainer. Consumers use other customers' reviews to help them make purchase decisions. So having lots of five-star reviews on your Amazon album pages can help boost sales. It's great if your fans post reviews on their own, but many will need some prodding from you. So ask them, and give them the exact Amazon web page where they can find your album and write glowing comments about it.

Reminder: Be sure to ask your fans to visit your pages at iTunes, CD Baby, etc., and post the same reviews on these sites, too.

Here are some other things you can do on Amazon.com whether or not you have music for sale on the site ...

#73

Create "Listmania" Lists

Amazon is all about empowering buyers to express themselves. That's why they allow anyone to create a "Listmania" list of favorite CDs, books and more on whatever topic or genre he or she chooses. The best thing to do to promote your music is create a list of top albums in your genre. The more specific, the better. For instance, if you play R&B

love songs, create a list called "Best R&B Love Song CDs" or "Top R&B Albums for Lovers."

If you have an album available on Amazon, put it at the top of the list. Of course! If you don't have a CD on Amazon, include the name of your act and your web site in some of the comments you write about each favorite album. A link to your Listmania list will sometimes show up on the pages of the albums you include on the list. This exposes you to other artists' fans, so be sure to include very targeted CDs on your list.

#74
Create "So You'd Like to ..." Lists

Similar to Listmania, "So you'd like to ..." lists allow Amazon customers to go into more detail about a particular hobby or interest, while still recommending albums and books available for sale on the site. Once again, your objective is to create a list that targets the people most likely to enjoy your music. So you might create "So you'd like to ... build an R&B love song collection" or "So you'd like to ... discover the best R&B love songs."

You can write a lot more comments with "So you'd like to ..." lists, so feel free to explain who you are, what you play, why you love your style of music, etc. Include your own album titles among your list of recommendations, as well as your web address.

I've found the exposure level of a "Listmania" or "So you'd like to ..." list has everything to do with how crowded the subject is. For example, a lot of people have lists on music business books. Therefore, my "So you'd like to ... Succeed as a Musician" list has only been viewed about 1,000 times. But my "So you'd like to ... Promote Your Creative Talents" page has been read more than 6,000 times. Fewer people have posted lists in that category.

So, the more specific you can be in an area not served by a lot of other lists, the better results you'll get.

#75

Write Amazon Customer Reviews

In addition to asking your fans to write reviews of your music, you can also benefit by writing your own reviews of other similar artists. This can be a powerful form of promotion on Amazon, especially if you are strategic with how you go about it.

What to do: Make a list of the top 10 or 20 albums you have opinions about whose fans overlap with your own music. Then one by one, write honest and insightful reviews of each album. After you post them, you will soon have a presence on the sales pages of other albums that attract your ideal music buyer.

You can't include web site addresses within a book review, but I have gotten away with ending my reviews with "-Bob Baker, author of Guerrilla Music Marketing Handbook."

Amazon may also allow you to reference why you're qualified to write about this genre – for instance, "As the lead singer of Marleyville, Detroit's most popular reggae band, I know a thing or two about Jamaican music in the Motor City ..."

Write thoughtful reviews of well-chosen albums, slip in subtle references to your name and location, and you will get more exposure. Also, don't overlook writing reviews of books that tie into your musical themes.

#76

Fill Out Your Amazon Personal Profile

Even if you never make your music available for sale on Amazon, you should make the most of the free Public Profile that Amazon gives everyone who creates an account.

On your public profile page you can post a photo, bio, personal interests, link to your web site, and other details related to your Amazon activities. Why do this? Because any time you post a product

review, a product photo, or any number of other things on the site, your name will appear with a live link to your Amazon profile. So be prepared and have it ready for potential music fans.

To update your Amazon profile, first create a free account at www.amazon.com, if you don't already have one. Once you're logged in, go to "My Account," then "Personalization" and "Your Public Profile." Click "Edit Your Profile" and fill in as many sections as possible.

It's amazing how many profile pages you can go to on Amazon and find virtually nothing on them – no photo, no bio, no web site link, nothing. Don't make this mistake! Fill out yours so at least some of the millions of active consumers who visit Amazon will know who you are, what you do, and how to find you.

#77

Make Good Use of Amazon's Secret "Signature" Field!

I refer to this as a "secret" field because most people – even those who are quite familiar with Amazon – overlook this simple but powerful element.

Look at any product review on Amazon and note what comes at the top after "By." You'll always see the reviewer's name. Sometimes you'll also find the name followed by some text in quotes. What shows in quotes is that person's Amazon "signature."

Most people use no signature at all, while some put silly descriptions such as "soccer mom" or "music lover." The best way to use a

> **Customer Review**
>
> 2 of 3 people found the following review helpful:
> ★★★★★ **Unleash the Professional Artist Within**, January 14, 2005
> By <u>Bob Baker "author, MusicMarketingBooks.com, FullTimeAuthor.com"</u>
> (Edit review) (Delete review)
> This review is from: **I Am A Professional Artist: The Key to Survival And Success in the World of the Arts (Paperback)**
> One of the best ways creative people can discover a blueprint for prosperity is to absorb and emulate the strategies of successful artists. Gilli Moon is one of those artists. In "I Am A Professional Artist," she bares her soul and shares the attitudes and actions it takes to make a true impact as a professional artist. Highly recommended!
>
> -Bob Baker, author of "Guerrilla Music Marketing Handbook" and "Unleash the Artist Within"

signature is to be descriptive (surprise!) and make good use of this valuable online real estate. Some musicians actually put "musician" as their signature. That's a good start, but you can do better.

I suggest you use either your band name or your web site as your Amazon signature.

Examples: Fred Jones "lead singer of Grind Shaft," or Fred Jones "GrindShaftMusic.com."

And remember, your name and signature appear wherever you post reviews on Amazon, which means your band name or web site will be in plain view for all to see. And if people click on your name, they are taken to your Amazon profile page, where they can learn even more about you. These are great tools, if you only use them!

To update your Amazon signature, go to "My Account," then scroll down to "Personalization." Click "Your Public Profile," then "Edit Your Profile."

Insight: See how this works? It's not just about what happens on your own album's sales page. The idea is to have *a presence across Amazon*, in all the places where your ideal fans are already surfing!

Okay, enough about Amazon. Let's move on to some other ways you can promote yourself and your music online ...

#78
Use These Directories to Find Record Stores

I don't advocate pursuing widespread retail distribution too early in your career. But once you have a buzz going in a particular region, it may make sense to get your physical CDs into select retail outlets. Use these sites to hunt down potential music sales locations – especially in cities where you tour and perform:

Worldwide Online Record Shops
www.moremusic.co.uk/links/world_sh.htm

Record Store Review
www.recordstorereview.com/links

Google Directory > Shopping > Entertainment > Recordings
directory.google.com/Top/Shopping/Entertainment/Recordings

#79

Find Thousands of Record Labels Online

These days, with the way the traditional music industry is crumbling, it's the Do-It-Yourself Era. So there's no real reason to ever get near a record label, in my opinion – except to watch an outdated business model struggle to stay alive.

But record labels still exist and potentially could serve a role in your musical future when the time is right. Use these web sites to hunt down record labels of all kinds – small, large and everything in between.

TAXI: Major and Indie Labels
www.taxi.com/members/links-labels.html

Google Directory > Music > Labels
directory.google.com/Top/Business/Arts_and_Entertainment/Music/Labels

All Record Labels
www.allrecordlabels.com

#80

Run Pay-Per-Click Ads Sparingly, if at All

I'll be honest with you. I've spent very little money on paid advertising throughout my entire career as an author. In the early days, it was out of necessity – I didn't have a budget for it at all. But as my business has grown, paid ads have remained low on my list of effective ways to promote and sell books.

Most independent musicians report the same results. Paid ads aren't all that effective, unless you run them repeatedly for months and years on end in the right places. Believe me, there are better ways to invest your limited resources.

Reality: Paid ads are the very last thing I recommend, but they are often the first thing that novice promoters think of when it comes to marketing. That's why this is one of the only sections in this book that will cover this topic.

If you're going to engage in some form of paid advertising, be smart about it. Use the most affordable methods and be strategic in your approach.

Strategy: One online advertising option you might consider is something called "pay per click." The name says it all: Your small line ad appears on various web sites, and you are only charged when someone clicks on it. Most of the pay-per-click programs also let you set a limit on how much you want to spend each month. When you reach that amount – whether it's $10 or $10,000 – your ads stop running until the start of the next month. This is a nice option for self-promoting musicians with small budgets.

The most popular pay-per-click program is Google AdWords. When you do a Google search, the results that appear in the wide column on the left are considered the "natural" or "organic" search results. Those little line ads that appear in the thin right column (and sometimes at the very top) and are labeled "Sponsored Links" are the pay-per-click ads.

Your goal is to come up in the organic search results on the left. But the next best thing is showing up among the Google AdWords listings, which you pay for using a bidding system. In essence, the more you are willing to pay per click, the higher your ad will appear in the column.

Yahoo, Microsoft and many other companies offer pay-per-click ad programs. Here are some links to help you research your options:

Google AdWords
adwords.google.com

Yahoo Search Marketing
searchmarketing.yahoo.com

Microsoft adCenter
adcenter.microsoft.com

BidVertiser
www.bidvertiser.com

There are entire books written about how to run effective pay-per-click campaigns. It is an art and a science. Read a book like *Pay Per Click Search Engine Marketing for Dummies* and do your homework before jumping into this paid ad arena.

#81

Consider These Newer Music Advertising Options

While Google was one of the first companies to pioneer making lots of money from thousands of small-budget advertisers using its AdWords program, many more prominent sites have seen the light and are now offering similar options. And some of them are geared specifically for music promotion.

Here are three promising ones in the low-budget category:

Jango Music Network
www.jango.com/advertise

Facebook Advertising
www.facebook.com/advertising

MySpace Ads for Musicians
www.myads.com/musicians.html

And here are four more prominent "music discovery" sites you can look into for advertising possibilities:

iLike
www.ilike.com/account/promoter_signup

Pandora
www.pandora.com

Grooveshark
www.grooveshark.com/advertising

Last.fm
www.last.fm/advertise

#82

Reach Highly Targeted Music Audiences

Here is yet another option ...

As you should know by now, my philosophy is all about targeting. You need to go directly to your ideal fans with your message. So if you must scratch the itch to spend money on ads, go for quality over quantity.

If there is a blog, web site, podcast, or email newsletter that reaches the ideal type of consumer for your music, contact the person who runs the site and see if they will accept a small fee from you each month in exchange for a sponsorship of some kind.

Better yet: Barter for the placement! If you have decent web traffic or a few thousand ezine subscribers, offer to swap exposure to each other's audiences. That way, you both win, and you don't have to spend a penny on advertising.

Again, go the paid advertising route only if you feel you absolutely have to. Believe me, it is not the miracle cure for obscurity.

But if you do use it, keep your ad budget low and your message targeted to the exact types of people you need to be reaching online.

In the next section: We demystify social networking and the interactive qualities of the online world.

Making the Most of Social Media and the Interactive Web

Now we dig deeper into Internet music promotion and get you even more actively involved in communicating with your fans. Use the many sites and tools covered in this section to further spread your music to the people who need to hear it the most.

#83

Understand What Social Networking Really Is

Is your head spinning with thoughts of Facebook, Twitter, MySpace, YouTube, Flickr, Tumblr, Foursquare, and countless other "social networking" web sites?

Well, relax. This section will put things in perspective and make it all easier to understand. By the time you finish reading the next few pages, you'll discover that social networking isn't so mysterious after all.

First, let's address the terms. The phrase "social networking" is simply a reference to the way people are interacting and communicating with each other online. That's all.

And the related phrase "social media" is just a way of describing all the multi-sensory online tools (text, audio, images, video, widgets, applications) that people are using to be "social."

Another odd phrase you may have heard is "Web 2.0." But don't worry. It's not a new software version of the Internet you have to upgrade to.

Definition: Web 2.0 is a term coined by O'Reilly Media, a computer book publisher that hosts an annual conference by that name. Web 2.0 is simply a way of describing a more interactive Internet, which evolved out of the static web sites of the past.

Even if you know all of this already, you may still be confused and overwhelmed by all there is to learn to promote your music effectively online. Again, relax. You don't have to know it all on day one. Chip away at the learning curve and absorb it little by little.

What's Really Going On Under the Hood?

When it comes to technological advances, you must remember one thing: Your focus should not be on the tools and the gadgets themselves. Your attention must stay on what's powering the technology. And the fuel that runs all of these electronic and digital systems is ... people.

That's right. Plain old human beings!

So, wrapping your head around "social networking" all boils down to understanding people. And here's the rock-bottom secret to it all:

Human beings are social creatures, and they have been for centuries. For generations, people have gathered in groups – the tribe, the town square, the corner bar, the family reunion, the gang at work, the sports team, the church picnic ... you name it.

People have a primal need to be around and communicate with other people – especially with those who share their outlook, interests and values. It's easy to get bogged down with ever-changing tech tools and file formats, but when you look under the hood, you'll see something that never changes: human nature at work.

Insight: Think of our basic need to communicate with each other as a body of water. It flows when and where it can. In the past, people were limited by geography and distance. You could only congregate with people in your immediate vicinity, unless you made the effort to travel to other places. Of course, in more recent decades, people made good use of snail mail and the telephone to connect, too. But ...

The Internet makes it possible to huddle up with like-minded people worldwide – without leaving home. Blogs, podcasts and video streams are simply the latest tools that allow people to express themselves and make connections with others – but now they're able to do so across the globe.

What an exciting time to be alive!

Truth: Ideas flow from person to person no matter what tools are available, but technology gives people more powerful options to share their messages with other humans.

So focus on the people aspect of this Internet marketing thing at all times. You have a special gift to deliver through your music. There are people around the globe who need to hear what you have

to say and play. Social media sites and interactive tools are simply the new pipelines to get your music delivered!

#84

Become a Consumer of the Technology First

Countless times I've had conversations with impatient musicians that go something like this ...

"Bob, I'm going to start my own blog soon and I really want to know how to use it to sell more music. What should I do?"

"Well," I reply, "what blogs do you subscribe to and read now?"

"Umm ..." he or she says, befuddled. "Actually, I don't read any. I've just heard that I should do one."

I understand their eagerness to jump into the online marketing waters. But when you think about it, this is a backwards approach.

Question: Would someone try to direct a film without ever having watched one? Or would an actor go audition for a play without ever having experienced live theatre?

Of course not. That would be like trying to write a song without ever having heard one!

Most likely, the thing that motivated you to play music in the first place was your consumption of other people's music. At some point you said, "I love that sound, and I bet I could learn to write and play that way too." And as you started to transform your ideas into sounds, you probably found yourself influenced by your favorite musicians' styles.

And that's a good thing. We all have people we admire who color how we approach a new craft until we find our own style and voice. The same thing is true of embracing new marketing tools and technologies.

Key: If you want to become a blogger, start reading what other bloggers are doing. First, look through the Technorati Top 100 Blogs list at www.technorati.com/blogs/top100 and subscribe to several of them. Also read the most prominent blogs by your favorite artists to see how your genre is being covered.

Once you do this for a while, you'll soon develop preferences and opinions. "I like the tone of her blog. He's too much of a self-promoter. That one is boring. Oh, I like that idea." Before long you'll formulate a solid idea of how you want your blog to look and feel.

Tip: This "become a consumer first" idea doesn't apply only to blogs. Take this same approach with podcasts, audio and video content, social networking sites, and more.

Yes, it takes a little more time to get acquainted with the landscape this way. But you'll be a much better informed and more effective musician if you become a consumer first, and a self-promoter second.

#85

Participate in Discussion Forums, Groups and Mailing Lists

To make the most of online social networking, you must be willing to be "social" and to "network." Again, this isn't about digital technology; it's all about human beings communicating with each other. And on the Internet, there are millions of conversations taking place at any given moment. As a self-promoting musician with value to share, you should be joining in on some of that dialogue.

There are thousands of ways to interact online, and we'll cover many of them in the pages that follow. One place to start is with discussion forums, groups and mailing lists – forms of Internet communication that have been in existence for many years and are still used extensively today.

This category of the social web basically has three formats:

1) Discussions that take place on a web page, where participants can view and respond to a topic thread,

2) Individual messages that are emailed to all "members" of the mailing list forum,

3) Or forums that combine both the web site and email components.

Two of the most popular sites that host such forums are:

Yahoo! Groups
groups.yahoo.com

Google Groups
groups.google.com

Go to either one of them and search for existing groups dedicated to hundreds of topics.

Here are some places to find music-specific forums:

Google Directory > Music > Chats and Forums
directory.google.com/Top/Arts/Music/Chats_and_Forums

Open Directory > Music > Chats and Forums
www.dmoz.org/Arts/Music/Chats_and_Forums

Topica – Music Channels
lists.topica.com/channels/music

It's time to reemphasize an important guerrilla music marketing concept: You must not concern yourself with the vast majority of these forums. Your only goal is to find groups that are in alignment with your music and message. And there are plenty of them, no matter what your genre.

For instance, there are forums and mailing lists for pharmacists, inventors, midwives, Mozilla software developers, Canadian nursing students, German translators, Scottish people who stutter, butch-femmes, Poicephalus Parrot owners, and more.

With this amazing diversity of online discussion, certainly there's a group out there for you!

To test this idea, I looked up discussion forums related to tango dancing, and quickly found the following:

Argentine Tango
www.tangoconnections.org

Tango Forum
www.topix.com/forum/music/tango

Tango Zone
groups.yahoo.com/group/atangozone

Dance Forums
www.dance-forums.com

There really is something out there for practically everyone.

The best way to make the most of these forums is to periodically check in and either start a topic or add to an existing discussion thread.

Important: Don't just post blatant "Hey, check out my music" remarks. Your goal is to truly add something useful to the discussion – even if it's only a short comment. Then include a blurb at the end as your "signature," such as:

```
Fred Jones
Acoustic music for nature lovers
www.MusicForNatureLovers.com
```

Tip: Being active on these forums can be time consuming, so be sure to identity the most potent ones. Pick two or three groups that are highly targeted and have an active membership, and place your efforts on them. That way, you'll become a recognized artist to the people who really matter: your ideal potential fans.

Get Familiar With Blogs and What They Can Do for You

Here's a quick primer on blogs and how you can use them to promote your music ...

As you may know, the word blog is short for "web log." A blog is basically an online journal that its author uses to publish "posts," which are separate entries to the journal. The term "blogosphere" merely refers to the ever-expanding collection of blogs across the Internet.

Blogs can be published for any reason and subject matter imaginable. From teenagers and activists to politicians and best-selling authors, anyone can easily and inexpensively publish a blog.

In many ways, blogs are just another version of a web site with multiple pages. You can visit and read a blog page in the same way you do any other web page. The main thing that sets a blog apart from a basic web page is a nifty Web-based file format called RSS.

Definition: RSS stands for Really Simple Syndication. In general, it is used to publish and organize frequently updated digital content, such as blogs, news feeds, and podcasts. The coolest thing about RSS is that it gives people the ability to subscribe to blogs and podcasts.

You can subscribe to blogs using something called a news reader, feed reader, or aggregator. These readers are popping up everywhere. The latest versions of the Firefox and Internet Explorer browsers allow you to subscribe to feeds directly from the browser.

You can also subscribe if you have a personalized page set up on Google, Yahoo or AOL. Or you can use programs and sites such as Bloglines, FeedDemon, and more.

Perspective: If you're not familiar with how these feed readers work, think about how your email inbox operates. You open your email program and up pops all of your latest incoming emails, listed by subject line, with the most recent message at the top.

Feed readers work in a similar way. Open it up, and all of the blogs you subscribe to will show up, with the latest content at the top, usually with just the headline and maybe the first few lines of the blog post displaying. It's a pretty convenient way to have only the information you want delivered to your desktop computer, laptop, or mobile phone.

#87
Find Blogs That Cater to Your Ideal Music Fans

Later we'll cover publishing your own blog. For now, let's focus on getting as much exposure as possible for your music on other people's existing blogs. The first thing you should do is track down the blogs that are already attracting your ideal type of fan.

Here are the two best blog directories to start your search:

Technorati Blog Directory
technorati.com/blogs/directory

Google Blog Search
blogsearch.google.com

Search both sites for words, phrases and topics related to your music.

#88

Leave Comments on Highly Targeted Music Blogs

Once you've compiled a list of targeted blogs, here is one simple thing you can start doing right away: Leave comments!

Most blogs allow you to post comments about each entry, and those comments do get read. Don't misuse this feature with "comment spam" that mindlessly hypes your music. Make sure your comment adds to or amplifies some aspect of the blog author's post. It's okay to make a sensible reference to your album or sound within your comment.

At the end of your comment, put your name and a link to your web site. Or, if the comment submission form has a field for your web site address, be sure to put it there.

#89

Send Useful Ideas and Links to Music Bloggers

One of your new online marketing goals should be to network with and get to know music bloggers. Search your favorite blogs for a Contact or About link that includes the email address of the blogger. Store these names and addresses in a database, then occasionally send them compliments, links to music sites that might interest them, or news about something you are working on.

Key: Your goal is to become a useful resource to bloggers, not a pest. That's why it's best to offer helpful ideas instead of just self-promotional messages. Reaching out to bloggers in this way will strengthen relationships with them and lead to some nice online exposure in the future.

#90

Uncover Blog Gold With Blogrolls

The term "blogroll" refers to a list of other blogs that bloggers recommend. You'll often find them in the right-hand column of your favorite blogs. Not every blog features them, but the ones that do can be very helpful in your hunt for the perfect blogs.

The reason they are so useful: Blogrolls act as filters that will save you time when researching and identifying blogs that cater to your music.

For instance, if you go to the Music Industry Report blog at www.MusicIndustryReport.org, you'll find links to a couple dozen of the best music business related blogs, including mine. If this was a music blog that catered to your exact genre and type of fan, this list would be invaluable.

So when you find a well-read blog that ideally covers your style of music, look to see if it features a blogroll and investigate those sites next. And if the best blogs on that list have blogrolls too ... you get the picture. Blogrolls can be great research tools.

#91

Get Familiar With Music Podcasts and Internet Radio

Now that you're comfortable with blogs and RSS feeds, let's dig into this phenomenon called podcasting. Even though the name was inspired by Apple's iPod, you don't need an iPod to either produce or listen to a podcast.

Definition: In essence, a podcast is an audio blog that features links to MP3 files (and sometimes video). An audio podcast can include music or spoken-word content and often features both. Think of it as a radio show that anyone with the right tools can produce and broadcast to the world.

Using the same RSS feed technology as blogs, people can subscribe to their favorite podcasts using a "podcatcher," a program that automatically downloads the latest media files from a selected list of podcasts to the subscriber's computer. Some popular podcatchers include iTunes, Odeo, PodNova, and Juice.

As you did with blogs, the first thing to do is uncover the best podcasts and online radio shows for your musical style. Here are some places to start your search:

Podcast Pickle
www.podcastpickle.com

Podcast Alley
www.podcastalley.com

iTunes
www.apple.com/itunes/store/podcasts.html

Podfeed
www.podfeed.net

Podcast Directory
www.podcastdirectory.com/format/Music

Okay. You're now armed with a hot list of podcasts that cater to your target audience. Now what? What follows are my top four podcast promotion ideas ...

#92

Send CDs or Links to Your Digital Album for Airplay

If a podcast or online radio show seems ideally in line with your musical genre or theme, offer to send your music to the host. If the Contact or About page includes a physical address, you could just blindly mail a copy of your CD. But it would be much better to email the host and ask if you can send one. That way there's an expectation that your music is on the way.

The same thing applies to emailing a link to your music online (which many podcasters prefer these days). Contact the host first and ask if he or she would like to sample your music and consider adding it to the show. You're always better off having some kind of communication exchange with someone instead of just throwing your stuff into "the void" and hoping someone sees it.

#93

Offer Yourself as a Podcast Guest

This is one angle that most musicians never think of. But since you now have a guerrilla music marketing mindset, you should be willing to open yourself up to the powerful possibilities this idea holds ...

Seek out podcasts and online radio shows that feature a talk-show format related to some aspect of your music. For example, if many of your fans use your music while they exercise, pitch yourself as a spokesperson for the health benefits of upbeat music. Some health- or even dance-related talk shows may have you on as a guest – and play some of your music while you're on.

Do you have a lot of knowledge of jazz or blues history? Could you speak intelligently about concert safety, or the effects of music on consumer spending in retail stores, or maybe the healing power of music? If you really think about it, you probably have expertise on some topic that would be of interest to talk show hosts.

How to get booked: Often it's as simple as sending an email to the host with a short bio and a pitch for why your music and unique perspective are worth covering. Be sure to offer a free review copy or link to your music. Emailing a teaser list of bullet point topics or suggested questions wouldn't hurt either.

#94

Submit Audio Comments

In a previous section on blogs (Tip #88), I suggested you leave intelligent comments. You can leave text comments on many podcast sites too. But a more creative option would be to record and send an audio response to something a podcaster covered on a recent episode. Just record it using your computer or a digital audio recorder and send an MP3 (or email a link to your audio file).

I guarantee you'll be one of the only people to submit comments this way, and many podcasters will appreciate you giving them extra content to include in their shows. The best part of it is: You will benefit from the extra exposure!

#95

Record Podcast Show IDs

You've heard these on commercial radio for decades. Well-known pop stars record short audio promo spots that mention a station's call letters. Well, this idea transfers easily to the podcast world as well.

Your recording might go something like this: "This is Dave Smith, lead singer for the Rockabilly Roadblasters, and you're listening to my favorite show, the Rockabilly Showcase Podcast." Easy, huh?

We'll cover more on how to create and publish your own audio content in Tips #109 and #110. For now, just know that existing podcasts and online radio shows offer potent ways to spread your music and message.

#96

Make Fabulous Friends With Facebook

How would you like to be part of a social networking site used by nearly one-fourth of all Internet users on the planet? That's the clout that Facebook.com can boast. Not bad for a site founded in 2004 by a few Harvard students who wanted to create a new way to interact with their friends.

There's a good chance you're already on Facebook. If not, you really should sign up for a free account ... *today!* If you are on Facebook, there's a good chance you're not using the site to its full potential to promote and sell your music.

Note that a full discussion on how to use this one site alone could take up volumes, so I'll only scratch the surface here. With that in mind, I will share my top five Facebook features you should be using to promote your music, starting with ...

A Personal Profile

This is the first step for everyone who joins Facebook. So if you're just getting started, spend some time beefing up your profile. (Note that this is for you as an individual, not your artist persona or entire band.) Definitely upload an appealing profile photo, then fill out the sections under "personal information."

Include details about your musical interests. Under "Arts and Entertainment: Music" and "Activities and Interests" include lots of references to similar artists. You can list more than one web site, so if you have separate addresses for your artist site, blog, Twitter account and so on, list them all.

Once your Facebook profile is in good shape, invite your friends and family to "friend" you, of course. Then take advantage of the feature that allows Facebook to access your email and search for people you know who are current members.

Important: At this point you should decide if you want to separate your personal life from your more public musical life. Some people choose to use their individual Facebook profile for family and close friends only; and create a "fan page" (which we'll cover next) for all their music promotion activities. However, some people choose to blend the two. It's your call.

#97

Create a Facebook Fan Page

The people who run Facebook are not dummies. They realized that a lot of members were using the site to promote themselves. So they created a special type of page for business purposes called Facebook Pages. To learn more about them, click the Home page link, then look in the far left column for a link titled "Ads and Pages." (You may need to click "more" to uncover it.) There you'll find a "Create Page" button.

Don't let the "Ads" reference fool you. Facebook Pages are free.

The main advantage to starting a separate fan page for yourself as a musician is the ability to send updates to all of your fans at once, no matter how many fans you have. With a personal profile, you can send messages to only 20 people at a time. (This is Facebook's way of keeping spammers from bulk mailing thousands of people at one time.)

Another perk: With a personal profile, you can have no more than 5,000 friends. That's not a problem for most people, but if you're a popular artist, you'll disappoint a lot of your fans when you reach your limit.

With a business/fan page, there is no cap on the number of fans you can have. That's why I recommend having both a personal profile and a fan page on Facebook.

Key: Even if someone is already on your email list or following you in some other way, you want them to connect with you on Facebook too. It's all about repetition and giving your fans lots of ways to stay in touch with you.

#98

Start a Facebook Group or Interact With Existing Ones

Here's another great interactive feature on Facebook: the ability to create forums dedicated to specific topics. There are two ways to use the Groups function. One is to seek out existing groups that are attracting the type of people who might enjoy your music.

Example: A search for "Grateful Dead" brought up many groups, one with more than 650,000 members.

But perhaps the best thing to do is start a Facebook group around the genre or theme of your music. Give it a specific, search-friendly name, like "Funk Fans Forum" or "The Blues Guitar Resource Center." Just make sure the group exists to foster lively discussions surrounding its genre and description, not just to serve as a place to post your music sales pitches.

Encourage members to start discussions, or post questions and invite replies. Again, the purpose is to get people involved in your topic or genre, while gently making them aware that you – as the founder of the group – are a musician with quality music to share as well.

#99

Post Facebook Events and Promote Them

When you present anything from an acoustic show at a coffee house to a major concert, Facebook is a great place to make people aware of your live events. To create an event listing, click the Home page link, then look in the far left column for an "Events" link next to a little red and white calendar icon that has a 31 in it. Once on that page, click the "Create an Event" button at the top.

Then just fill out all the event details: date, time, location, address, description, etc. Once your event is created, you can invite people on your friends list to attend. One cool feature Facebook offers is the ability to filter the people you invite by their location – so, for example, you can select just everyone on your friends list who lives in Chicago and invite them only.

Tip: You can also use Facebook to invite people to virtual events, such as performances that are broadcast live using streaming video. Just type something like "Anywhere you have access to a computer" in the Location field.

#100
Use These Facebook Music Applications

One thing there's no shortage of on Facebook is the number of gizmos, games and applications you can add to your profile or fan page and share with your friends. While a lot of these things can be fun, I encourage you to be very strategic as you choose which ones to add and use. Sure, you can "throw sheep" at people and send silly quizzes, but always ask yourself, "Why?"

Important: The best applications serve a purpose! They engage your audience or pull in useful content that otherwise resides outside of Facebook. Apps that pull in your music, videos or photos are potentially good ones. Also, if you can integrate your activity on Twitter or your blog using an app, that's worth considering.

There are a number of applications designed for artists to showcase their stuff. Here are six prominent ones:

ReverbNation's Band Profile
www.facebook.com/rn.mybandapp

Nimbit's Music – MyStore
apps.facebook.com/nimbitstore

iLike
www.facebook.com/iLike

RootMusic
www.rootmusic.com

Moontoast Impulse
www.fanimpulse.com

Pagemodo
www.pagemodo.com

As I mentioned, these tips only briefly touch on how you can use Facebook to promote and sell music. The main thing to know is that Facebook is big and growing bigger every month. So stay active on the site as you make new friends and turn many of them into fans.

#101
Use Twitter to Tweet Your Message to the Masses

You've no doubt heard of Twitter, one of the fastest growing social sites going in recent years. It's often referred to as a "micro-blogging" platform because of the minimalist nature of how people use it – to post short messages of no more than 140 characters long (including spaces). The messages can be sent, received and read on mobile phones and regular computers via special applications or the Twitter web site.

Messages you post to Twitter are referred to as "tweets." You can keep track of tweets posted by people you choose to "follow."

Likewise, people who want to track your activities can do so by clicking the "follow" button on your Twitter profile page.

Twitter is by far the easiest and quickest way to get involved in social networking. It takes minutes to set up an account, upload a photo, and add a short bio and a link to your web site. And, with a 140-character maximum, it takes no time to craft a message to post. In fact, you'll spend more time editing your thoughts down to one or two quick sentences than you will thinking of something to say.

The site was originally created to help its users answer that probing question, "What are you doing?"

For better or worse, many users have taken this theme to heart by letting others know everything they're doing – and I mean everything! Common messages report such meaningful activities as "Stopping to get gas and buy a pack of cigs" or "Running late for the photo shoot" or "It's raining outside and I'm bored."

Is Twitter Worth the Time?

That's the most common response when someone is exposed to Twitter for the first time. "And I need to be on this time-wasting site ... why?"

I don't blame you for wondering. So let me explain it this way: Consider the cell phone. Would you agree that a lot of people use cell phones for idle, mindless chatter? (Insert your own personal teenager

107

reference here.) Of course they do. But does that mean that cell phones are never used for constructive purposes?

Can you think of a time when you used a cell phone to close a business deal or simply get directions or reach someone with important, timely information? I'm sure you can.

Think of Twitter (and all of these new online tools) in the same light. No doubt, many people will use them for nonsensical purposes. But a lot of smart people (including musicians and music promoters) have figured out ways to leverage them for maximum personal and business advantage.

Twitter success stories: Amanda Palmer of the Dresdon Dolls generated $19,000 in music merchandise sales in a 10-hour period using Twitter and a silly T-shirt idea. Rapper Mack Maine posted a link to his new mixtape track on Twitter, which led to 14,000 downloads in 48 hours.

Of course, you most likely won't get results on that scale. But they give you an idea of what's possible.

Musicians should use Twitter to alert fans about live shows, new free download samples, new blog posts, media coverage, where their singles and albums can be purchased, and more.

A Word of Warning

While I encourage you to be strategic with your Twitter and other social networking activities, I also want to caution you against coming across as too sales-oriented. If all you ever do is post promotional announcements, your followers will tune you out or, even worse, "unfollow" you. And that's where injecting some of your personal life can be a good thing.

No, I don't need to know what you have for lunch every day. But if you discover a great new restaurant, that might be worth tweeting about. I don't need to know that you can't sleep and are bored. But you can present it along with a meaningful question, like "Having trouble sleeping. What's your best cure for insomnia?"

It's all about finding a balance between useful information, subtle self-promotion, and insightful peeks into your life and personality.

While you can't squeeze a lot of information into those 140 characters, you can and should use Twitter to send your followers to sites and resources throughout the Internet.

Here's a quick list of links that a guerrilla music marketer might tweet about:

- Links to your latest music video or blog post
- Links to instant photos you post from your smartphone using a free service like Twitpic (www.twitpic.com) or Instagram (www.instagr.am).
- Links to talented musicians who open for you or that you discover during your travels
- Links to articles or blog posts not written by you that might be of interest to your fans

Tip: Many links will be too long to fit into your short tweets. In such cases, use a free URL shortener site such as www.bit.ly or www.tinyurl.com.

Here are seven more Twitter topic ideas with examples of actual tweets I've posted:

- **Requests for help to solve a problem**: "I need to improve how I manage my time. What tools do YOU use to set priorities and get things done?"

- **Questions to stimulate conversation**: "On a scale from 1 to 10, where are you operating today? And why?"

- **Quick tips and observations**: "Love the new Task box in Gmail. Got a lot done using it this week. But ... it's not the tool, it's your personal focus that matters!"

- **Teasers about upcoming projects**: "Editing a new podcast – my interview with Joe Vitale. Should be posted soon."

- **Tweets about unusual personal experiences**: "Just obliterated 2 hornets nests under the table on our deck (got stung 4 times last week). It had to be done."

- **Inspiring quotes**: "I couldn't wait for success, so I went ahead without it." -Jonathan Winters

- **Personal updates that reinforce credibility**: "Just had a great chat session with my Berklee music marketing students."

This isn't spleen surgery. It's just making smart use of new technology. With so many people jumping on the Twitter wagon, it makes sense for you to be there too. So hop on board and start giving your fans tidbits of info they can use – while cementing your reputation as an active and interesting artist.

#102

Use Video to Spread Your Music on YouTube and Beyond

As a musician who creates art with sound, you are understandably focused on getting people to *hear* what you create. And that's a smart thing to do, of course. But as a self-promoting musician online, it's also very important these days to connect with fans through the visual senses as well. So you need to incorporate video into your online guerrilla marketing plans.

Internet video is a powerful medium. Many millions of people around the world watch millions of videos online every day. And they're viewing them increasingly on their mobile phones, as well as on regular computers.

This is a growing trend you should definitely embrace. But I recommend you do it not simply because you can, but because using video is yet another way to engage your audience and communicate who you are and what you offer as a musician.

Enter the YouTube Kingdom

There are now many video hosting sites across the Web, but the granddaddy of them all is YouTube (www.youtube.com), which at last count was serving up some 100 million videos a day to its users.

How it works: Once you register for a free YouTube account (be sure to select a Musician Account), you can upload video clips of 15 minutes or less (up to two gigabytes in size) in a variety of formats. The site then converts them to a streaming format that people can view on the YouTube site itself or embedded on other web sites. There's a lot of competition for attention on YouTube, but some videos rise to the top and are seen by millions of people.

While YouTube is the king, there are many other video hosting and sharing sites where you can upload your videos, including these:

Blip.tv
www.blip.tv

Vimeo
www.vimeo.com

Revver
www.revver.com

Dailymotion
www.dailymotion.com

Joost
www.joost.com

#103

Create Video Content That Will Engage Your Fans

Regardless of which video site you choose to use, here are six ways to make the most of online video:

- **Don't let a low budget stop you.** If you're sweating because you think your video content has to be a big-budget extravaganza, slap some cold water on your face right now. In this modern era, it's more about the idea behind the visuals than it is the production quality.

  Granted, it helps to have a nice camera and editing software (and the skills to use them tastefully). But many people have received widespread exposure using only a $50 webcam on their home computer.

- **Think outside the format box**. On YouTube and other similar sites, videos come in many different forms. They can be as simple as single-camera shots of you performing in your living room or on a stage, or as complex as full-blown, MTV-style music videos.

  But I encourage you to think low budget at first. Record your rehearsal or studio sessions, shoot footage of life on the road, or capture the interactions you have with your fans. As long as you're sharing some part of yourself with your readers, it's all fair game.

- **Develop your profile page**. YouTube (and just about every social media site, for that matter) allows you to design a profile page that contains links to all of your videos, a short bio, and a link to your artist web site. People can also subscribe to your "channel" and get updates whenever you post new video content. You want to encourage this connection. And while you're at it, subscribe to and leave comments on other music video producers' work, which will cause your name to appear on their pages.

- **Elicit a strong reaction for maximum effect**. There are no sure-fire recipes for creating a popular "viral" video. But I have noticed that the most-viewed online videos have some common traits. The main element they share: inspiring a physical or emotional response from viewers.

  In other words, if you can get someone to laugh or cry or be moved in some meaningful way by a video clip, you increase the chances that he or she will tell someone else about it. So think about the emotional impact you can add to your videos before you create them.

- **Keep them short**. People are busy. Attention spans are getting shorter as Web surfers learn to quickly scan and filter out what they will and won't spend time on. You might be tempted to treat people to your 10-minute exploration of Jimi Hendrix guitar solo techniques. But it would be much better for your viewers if you kept your clips to three or four minutes – or less!

Editing tip: Most computers come with free video editing software these days. If you have a PC, look for Windows Movie Maker. If you work on a Mac, you may have a free copy of iMovie.

Uploading shortcut: Since uploading large video files can take a bit of time, most people don't want to mess with starting accounts at multiple video-sharing sites. However, you should be aware of TubeMogul (www.tubemogul.com), a site that will upload your videos to several popular sites at the same time.

#104
Use Video to Inspire Fan Interaction

Okay. You want your videos to be found on YouTube and other video sites. Another cool thing is that these services usually give you the HTML code to "embed" your videos on your own web site. Your fans can also embed them on their blogs, etc. That's all great.

But there's another way to use video that most musicians don't even consider. However, since you have a guerrilla marketing mindset, you will now open your mind to the possibility of using this powerful tactic.

I'm talking about creating video clips that are to be specifically used on your web site as welcome messages, greetings, and calls to action.

Here are some examples:

- **Home page welcome message**. When fans come to your web site for the first time, wouldn't it be nice if you give them the option of watching a special video message from you: "Hi. Thanks so much for visiting my web site. Here you'll find ..."

- **Email sign-up page greeting**. I've already stressed the importance of building an email list and how you should create incentives for fans to sign up. Add some extra muscle to those efforts with a short video clip on your mailing list sign-up page. You might say, "I have so many exciting projects coming up, and I don't want you to miss out on all the free demo downloads I'll be giving away. So please take a moment right now to fill in your name and email address in the form below ..."

- **Sales page explanation video**. When fans click to your music sales page, give them more than a list of your albums and where they can buy them. Place a video at the top that explains the different options and helps them choose the best collection of songs for their needs.

I've always admired the way Jana Stanfield uses video on her music web site. Watch her message to meeting planners at www.janastanfield.com/live.

#105
Stream Live With These Free Video Sites

You may have noticed that the digital world we live in is feeding the human desire for instant gratification. We want information, music, books, movies, and games ... and we want them now! And more increasingly, we can get what we want online right away. Hence, the instant download.

In the video world, the latest extension of that trend is the ability to stream video live – as it happens. No waiting to shoot, convert, edit and upload the file. Just hook up your webcam and log on to one of the free streaming video sites, and you're ready to broadcast live to the world – of course, you still have to attract an audience.

There are many ways musicians can use this technology, such as: broadcast your live shows, offer a "studio cam" while you are recording, hold question and answer sessions for your fans, etc.

Here are three of the top streaming video sites:

Ustream.tv
www.ustream.tv

Stickam
www.stickam.com

Justin.tv
www.justin.tv

As you can see, there are countless ways to employ video in your online music promotion efforts. So pick an idea, grab a camera, and become your own instant indie film producer.

#106

Claim (or Reclaim) Your Music Space on MySpace

At one time (way back in 2006 or so), MySpace.com was the social networking powerhouse and poster child. Musicians and other creative people flocked to it in its early years and brought a lot of their fans with them. In more recent years – with the rise of Facebook,

Twitter and more – MySpace has lost the buzz-worthy edge it once had.

However, the site has more than 100 million users and is still widely known as a music destination. Therefore, if you are a self-promoting musician of any kind, you really should have a profile there. And if you already have a MySpace artist page, you should update it and check in from time to time. (The reason I mention this is because many artists I know have abandoned their MySpace profiles in favor of spending more time on Facebook and other sites. It's fine to shift your priorities, but don't completely turn your back on MySpace.)

Here are my top three quick tips on making the most of MySpace:

- **Update the look and layout of your profile**. One of the early highlights of MySpace was the ability to customize the look of your profile page. This also became part of its downfall, since so many people with no design skills or taste created bloated pages that made it hard to navigate the site.

  Well, MySpace still gives you a lot of flexibility to design (for better or worse) your artist profile page, but it now offers Profile 2.0. This feature allows you to choose pre-designed templates and layout options that look appealing without bombarding your senses or bandwidth. Visit www.myspace.com/profileeditor for more details.

- **Require your approval before comments are posted**. Another sad thing about MySpace is the amount of "band spam" that permeates the site – from your inbox to your profile page itself. You don't need your page being cluttered with dozens of bands yelling "Hey, check me out!" So go into your account settings and make sure it's set to require your approval before any new comments are posted. That way, only relevant things from your fans will show up on your page.

- **Seek out "active" fans of similar artists**. Make a list of the top five to ten artists whose fan base overlaps with yours. Find their MySpace pages and friend them. Then, as time allows, look for the fans who are leaving genuine comments on those artists' pages. Send them a personal message, like "I see you're a fan of [name]. Love the comment you left about [details]. Just wanted to let you know I write and record music that is often compared to [name]. Take a listen and decide for yourself at [myspace address or your artist web site]."

Beyond that, check in once or twice a week and respond to new messages, approve comments, add new gigs to the calendar, post bulletins, maybe even post a new blog update. Whatever you do, don't completely abandon MySpace. At least not yet.

#107
Publish Your Own Blog to Engage Fans and Help Search Engines Find You

In an earlier section (Tips #86 through #90) I covered what blogs are and how to promote your music through existing blogs run by other people. In this section I will encourage you to also consider publishing your own blog.

Why? Here are four things your own blog can help you accomplish:

- **Develop a following**. When you create new content on a regular basis, you give fans a reason to reconnect with you and your music time and time again. A static web site offers no incentive for repeat exposures.

- **Create promotional tentacles**. You know by now that Internet music marketing is all about outreach and creating a trail of topic-specific breadcrumbs that lead readers to your web site.

Every time you publish a new post to your blog, you create yet another trail that your ideal fans can find.

- **Earn better search result positions**. Google and other search engines love blogs because it gives them more content to categorize, and it demonstrates which sites are active and growing. The more active and relevant your blog is, the greater your chances of ranking higher in Google search results.

- **Create interaction and community with your fans**. Most bloggers allow readers to leave comments. That's another thing that sets blogs apart from static web pages: people can interact with them. You should encourage and ask your readers to leave comments. That will make your blog a place that fans will want to visit often and express themselves at while there.

How to Publish Your Own Blog

The great news about blogs: There are many services out there that make it easy to publish one. Here are five popular services to consider:

Blogger
www.blogger.com
A free service owned by Google. Very easy to set up and use. Just choose a template and go. This is what I use for my blogs.

WordPress
www.wordpress.org and www.wordpress.com
A popular open-source blogging platform that has grown tremendously in recent years. Offers both free and paid versions.

Posterous

www.posterous.com

A cool blogging platform that makes it easy to share text, photos, audio, and video across all of your social sites. I really like this one!

Tumblr

www.tumblr.com

Another easy blog creation site that is similar to Posterous and growing in popularity.

Six Apart

www.sixapart.com

A company that offers multiple free and paid online journal options, including TypePad, Moveable Type, and Vox.

Tip: FeedBurner (www.feedburner.com) is a free service that can help you streamline your RSS feed subscriptions, add interactivity, and include lots of cool features. Use it in combination with one of the blog services above.

#108

Use a Blog to Promote and Sell Your Music

If you already publish a blog or are about to start one, congratulations! You're miles ahead of many other musicians. Now here are several ways you can turn your blog into an online music marketing machine:

- **Deliver your news, your way.** The most basic thing you can do with a music blog is announce your activities: live shows you have scheduled, new songs and albums you've released, awards you've won, media coverage you've just landed, etc. Let people know about all of your music-related activities. But there are other things you should do with your blog too. So read on ...

- **Share your creative journey**. A blog can be part personal diary, part "making of" documentary. Invite fans to follow along as you log reports about your adventures through the writing, recording and performing world. Post daily dispatches from the road, keep fans updated on your creative process, or tell them about the great show you gave the night before. Share yourself with your fans and they'll feel more of a connection with you.

- **Post often**. Some bloggers publish something every day; others post entries once or twice a week. Choose a frequency that works for you and do your best to stick with it.

I suggest at least one post a week; more if you can swing it. What you want to avoid is DBS (Dead Blog Syndrome) – where weeks or months go by between posts. Lifeless blogs don't get read … and won't help you promote and sell music!

- **Report on your musical genre**. Here's an idea that could bring you a lot of targeted traffic. Instead of publishing a blog that promotes you and your music only, create one that acts as a one-stop resource for your entire genre.

For example, if you write and record love ballads, start the Love Ballad Blog. Publish reviews and links to your favorite love song-related artists, albums and web sites. You just might attract a lot of incoming traffic from people searching for the genre. Of course, you can include plenty of plugs for your own music, but the main focus of the blog will not be on you alone.

- **Extend link love**. There's a lot of cross-referencing that takes place in the blog world. You should regularly scour the Web for news and online resources that would be of interest to your fans. Then write about (and link to) those other blogs, sites, artists, etc.

  After you publish a new post, send a quick email to the person whose site you plugged. This will often lead to a return link when that webmaster or blogger writes about the exposure they got on your blog. The best way to get link love is to give it unconditionally in the first place.

- **Make your blog post titles sizzle**. Compare the titles you give your blog posts to the headlines that appear on magazine covers. How do they rate? What's more likely to get one of your readers to click a link to read your latest entry: "Interesting Story" or "You'll Never Believe What I Found in My Shoe This Morning"? Take time to craft the best, attention-grabbing titles you can.

- **Promote new music projects as you create them**. Instead of waiting for your entire new CD to be released, you can start marketing a new album the day you decide to create it. Throughout the creation of her album *Ellipse*, Imogen Heap posted regular video blog updates for her fans, which led to North American chart success and two Grammy nominations when the album was released.

We've only scratched the surface of how to use your own blog to promote and sell more music. But if you take the steps outlined on these pages, you'll have a great head start in the blog world.

#109

Create Your Own Podcast to Make Connections and Sell Music

Have you ever dreamed of hosting your own radio show? Many musicians have. It's an alluring idea. When you produce your own podcast online, it's like having your own audio program – and, for some guerrilla music marketers, it can be an effective promotion tool.

The good news: A podcast takes more technical skills to publish than a simple text-based blog. And for the average person, it can be daunting to get familiar with microphones, audio editing software, bit rates, etc. But since you're an active musician, there's a good chance you already have some experience and skills in this area, which will make podcasting easier for you.

However, to be effective with it and build an audience, just know that you will need to produce shows on a regular schedule. The first few are often easy to crank out. But ... can you sustain that enthusiasm over the long haul?

If so, your first step is to learn the technical requirements of recording, editing, uploading, and promoting your show. I won't go into all those details here, but I will direct you to these two helpful resources that will shed light on podcasting:

How to Podcast Tutorial
www.how-to-podcast-tutorial.com

How to Create a Podcast
www.youtube.com/watch?v=-hrBbczS9I0

As podcasting has grown, so have the number of services available to help you host and manage your audio files. Here are four podcasting sites that offer a range of free and paid service options:

Blog Talk Radio
www.blogtalkradio.com

Podbean
www.podbean.com

Libsyn
www.libsyn.com

Audio Acrobat
www.audioacrobat.com

#110
Add Promotional Punch to Your Podcast

Once you have your own podcast up and running, here are some ideas on how to use it to promote and sell your music:

- **Share your newest songs, demos and more**. This is the obvious way to make the most of your own podcast: Be sure to feature your music on it! Play some or all of certain tracks from your current and previous albums, and let listeners know where they can purchase them. Also share song ideas you're working on, demo recordings, and alternate studio takes.

- **Play live versions of your songs**. Get in the habit of recording all of your live gigs. Pick some of the best performances and play them on your podcast. Also feature any amusing stories or stage banter from live events, or interactions you had with fans.

- **Add spoken-word commentary**. Highlighting your songs on a podcast is smart, but so is including some messages from you speaking directly to your listeners and fans. Treat it like your own talk and music show. Relate funny stories or what inspired you to write various songs or what happened behind the scenes the day of a recording session. Have some fun with it!

- **Become a genre resource**. Here's a concept: Base your podcast theme around your musical genre. Play other independent artists your fans will enjoy (with the artist's permission, of course) in addition to your own music. This idea alone could dramatically expand your listener base.

- **Use an interview format**. Ask a friend or a journalist to do audio interviews with you. Or you can play interviewer and invite other artists to be your guests. Record interviews in person when you attend events or long distance over the phone. Conversations are often more interesting than a solitary voice.

- **Write attention-getting show titles**. Make sure the name you give each episode is riveting and filled with rich keywords. I'm not talking about how you describe it on the recording. I'm referring to the headline you use on the episode's podcast web page.

  For example, "What a Week It's Been" is not a strong headline. "How I Ended Up in Handcuffs in the Back of a Police Car" would grab a lot more attention. Be specific, mysterious, outrageous, or funny with your titles ... just don't be dull.

- **Edit your ID3 tags**. These tags supply the information in an MP3 file that is displayed when your audio is played on an iPod or other digital media player. The most important tags are Title, Artist and Album. Don't leave these blank. You want people to know what they're listening to long after they've downloaded your podcast episode. (A free Windows program that can help you do this is MP3tag at www.mp3tag.de/en.)

If your show is called the Radical Reggae Podcast, your Title tag should be something like "RRP 10 – Why Ziggy Marley Matters." Include a standard abbreviation and show number, followed by the episode title.

For the Artist tag, put your name and web site: "Rasta Robbie - RastaRobbie.com." In the Album tag slot, spell out the full name of the podcast. Taking these steps will ensure that fans are able to store and find your files quickly, and they can get in touch with you when they want.

No doubt about it: Creating your own podcast offers a potentially powerful way to promote and sell music online.

#111
Post Your Pics on Flickr and Other Photo Sharing Sites

With all the interactive capabilities on the Web these days, digital still photos may seem quite "old school." But don't dismiss the power of your pictures and the opportunity that photo-sharing sites offer to increase your online presence.

Keep in mind how important it is to leave a trace of yourself and your message in many places where lots of people are gathering online. While YouTube, Facebook and Twitter may grab more headlines, there are many millions of people who still actively surf the photo sites. Therefore, you should be there.

Here are three reasons to post your pictures on photo-sharing sites:

- **Enhance your credibility**. Images show you in action doing what you do. Yes, your music should speak for itself, but offering visual images that your fans and supporters can enjoy adds another layer of credibility to your career. But you must be strategic in how you do this.

  So, post photos of you on the stage, in the studio, and on the road. If you write songs about fast cars, show yourself behind the wheel of a sports car. If you support a children's charity, display shots of you volunteering. Capture the interesting things you encounter along your musical journey and share them with others online.

- **Expand your reach**. These photo sites obviously give you a place to upload and store your digital pictures. That means, if you want to use them on your blog or web site, you can simply link to your images on the hosting site instead of messing with uploading them to your own web server.

  More importantly, most of these sites give you badges, widgets and feeds that allow you to share your photo "stream" on other popular web sites. That means you upload images to one site but can share them across several sites.

- **Connect with celebrities**. I love attending conferences and events and meeting people I admire, including celebrities. I've had my picture taken with Alec Baldwin, Jack Canfield, Rev. Michael Beckwith, Tavis Smiley, Dr. Ruth Westheimer, and many more. I post these photos online, which adds to my credibility by association. You should do the same.

- **Feature your album cover and more**. In addition to uploading photos of yourself and the people you meet, you can also post images of your album covers, promotional materials, etc.

I discovered the benefit of this by accident when I uploaded the cover of one of my books to Flickr. Some weeks later,

I searched for the title on Google and the book cover's Flickr page came up high in the results. I also uploaded a web page screen shot of my *Guerrilla Music Marketing Handbook* when it hit #1 in the Music Business book category on Amazon. What images display your success? Whatever they are, post them now.

- **Spread more "link bait" around.** The key to making the best use of photo sharing sites is giving your images precise titles and descriptions. Load them up with the keywords that your ideal fans may use to find music that interest them online.

  For example, with the book cover image I mentioned earlier, I didn't simply title it "book cover." I labeled it "55 Ways to Promote & Sell Your Book on the Internet." That's why it came up in a Google search, and that's how it acts as another tentacle that helps people discover me on the Internet.

128

Tip: When it comes to places that host still photos on the Web, Flickr (www.flickr.com) is king of the heap. Millions of people post and tag their images on this mega site, which was purchased by Yahoo a few years ago. From animals and architecture to water and weddings, you'll find it here. Flickr has free and paid accounts with different feature levels. It's the main photo site in which I suggest you invest your time.

But there are other online image hosting sites you should explore as time allows. Here are three more:

Photobucket
www.photobucket.com

Shutterfly
www.shutterfly.com

Picasa Web Albums
picasaweb.google.com

Bottom line: Your music may be primarily comprised of sound. But when it comes to promoting it online, don't overlook how you can reinforce your message visually.

#112

Use Tagging and Bookmarking Sites to Generate Web Traffic

There are more people surfing the Web and more stuff available to read, hear and see than ever before. It's a crowded, noisy Internet. So how do people find the things that are most relevant to them? Of course, search sites like Google are one of the most common ways that consumers discover things. But another method people use to filter through the clutter is something called "tagging."

If you've ever used web sites like YouTube, Flickr or Delicious, you may already be familiar with tagging. It takes place when someone posts a new photo, video or favorite link on one of these sites and then gives it a descriptive "tag" – one or more words that describe what it is.

Example: If you publish a picture on Flickr taken during your trip to the Grand Canyon, you might give it tags such as "Grand Canyon, Arizona, vacation, hiking."

The important thing about tags on most of these social media sites is this: You aren't the only one who can see and use your tags. Anyone who visits Flickr can search the entire site for photos tagged "Grand Canyon" or "hiking."

And you can quickly find out who else is posting Grand Canyon photos too. This allows you to find other people with similar interests and for them to find you. It's targeted interaction on an extremely personal level.

Using Bookmarking Sites to Promote Your Music

A related trend is referred to as "bookmarking." In essence, bookmarking web sites exist to give people a public place to log and share their favorite links. And guess what? Most of these sites ask users to "tag" their links with descriptive words and phrases too. Which makes these sites great places to find your ideal fans and for them to find you.

When it comes to the bookmarking realm, here are the two most prominent sites:

Delicious
www.delicious.com

Founded in 2003, Delicious is considered one of the first major social bookmarking services. It allows users to tag, save, share and discover web pages from a centralized source. The site, now owned by Yahoo, has more than five million users and 150 million bookmarked URLs.

StumbleUpon
www.stumbleupon.com

This prominent site is an Internet community of more than 14 million people that allows its users to discover and rate web pages, photos and videos. According to the site, "As you click Stumble!, we deliver high-quality pages matched to your personal preferences. These pages have been explicitly recommended by your friends or … other web surfers with interests similar to you."

Hopefully, you understand the potential power of tapping into these existing online communities. While Delicious and StumbleUpon are considered the two main sites in the bookmarking category, there are others, such as:

Diigo
www.diigo.com

Clipmarks
www.clipmarks.com

eSnips
www.esnips.com

More About Tagging …

It's one thing to "bookmark" a favorite link on one of these sites. But it doesn't become useful to you or the community until it is "tagged." This is how Delicious defines what a tag is:

"A tag is simply a word you can use to describe a bookmark. Unlike folders, you make up tags when you need them and you can use as many as you like. The result is a better way to organize your bookmarks and a great way to discover interesting things on the Web."

Key lesson: The best way to use tagging to promote your music is to think about the words that fans of your genre or style use most when searching for stuff online. Then make sure you bookmark lots of links that would be of interest to those types of people, and tag them accordingly.

For example, when bookmarking a link to a helpful music marketing article, I tag it with a variety of words and phrases: music marketing, music promotion, band promotion, music sales, promote my music, etc. I think about the words that my ideal fans might use to search for this type of information. By including a variety of word combinations in my tags, I increase the likelihood that the right reader will connect with me.

The same thing goes for links a heavy metal guitar player might post. Those tags might include: heavy metal, hard rock, speed metal, shred, etc. The more descriptive the tags, the greater the odds that your ideal fans will find you.

Does this make sense?

Great. Then get busy using bookmarking and tagging to reach even more of your ideal fans online!

#113

Tap Into the Power of Social News Sites

There's another breed of bookmarking site that is focused more on news-related links. Consider starting free accounts on these sites too and use them to extend your online reach:

Digg
www.digg.com

Newsvine
www.newsvine.com

Mixx
www.mixx.com

reddit
www.reddit.com

Yahoo! Buzz
buzz.yahoo.com

#114

Use LinkedIn to Make Business Connections and More

The terms "social media" and "social networking" are often applied to a wide range of web sites. But you may have noticed that each of the destinations in this broad category have unique characteristics that color how they are used. If you think of it in terms of your physical world, Facebook might be the corner bar you go to for happy hour. MySpace would be the live music venue. To continue the analogy, LinkedIn would be your local business association.

Don't think that LinkedIn is only for corporate types and white collar cubicle dwellers. People from all industries and walks of life are interacting on this popular site – including indie musicians, producers, concert promoters, booking agents, venue owners, and people who run music companies of all kinds. If you're not on LinkedIn yet, you should consider starting an account soon.

Here are several tips for making the most of LinkedIn:

- **Complete your profile**. As is the case with most of these social sites, filling out your profile page is crucial. Just because LinkedIn is a business-centric site with a resume profile format, that doesn't mean your descriptions have to be serious and dry. I encourage you to show your personality and make your profile sing with an intriguing and interesting story.

  Make sure the short headline that appears prominently below your name is clear, descriptive and catchy. Also spend time fleshing out the Summary section and list a lot of keywords related to what you do in the Specialties area. Don't use the generic "My website" to describe the link to your personal site. Be descriptive: "My salsa dance music site."

- **Consider a company profile too**. In the same way that Facebook offers both personal profiles and business pages, LinkedIn offers similar options as well. If you run a recording studio or label, or just want to set up a separate page for your band or artist identity, a company profile may be a good option for you.

- **Join targeted groups**. Most social media sites these days give users opportunities to huddle up with like-minded individuals. That's why a lot of active LinkedIn users make good use of the Groups area. Click the "Groups" tab when you're logged in and search for existing groups related to your musical genre, lyrical themes, etc. Join a few of the more active ones you find, then contribute to the discussions taking place.

  If you don't find many LinkedIn groups to your liking, then start one of your own. To learn more about Groups and how they work, visit learn.linkedin.com/groups.

- **Use the search feature**. Of course, the main reason to use LinkedIn is to get "linked" to others in your musical category. The People Search function can help you locate ideal

134

connections. Use the "Advanced" search feature to find people by keyword, company, industry, city, and more.

- **Give and get recommendations**. This is a cool feature unique to LinkedIn. The best way to start is to "recommend" other people you enjoy and admire. Scroll through their profile and click the "recommend" link below the job title that applies. Doing this will create goodwill. After a while you can also encourage others to recommend you. And since these glowing comments appear on your LinkedIn profile page, the more you have, the better you look.

- **Ask questions, give answers**. Another great LinkedIn feature is its "Answers" function. Want to know what the best music publicity contacts are in Seattle? Post the question on LinkedIn and tap into your community for answers. Likewise, look over other people's questions and answer the most relevant ones. Visit www.linkedin.com/answers for more info.

- **Promote your events**. Yes, LinkedIn even has a place to post your events too. So you might as well use it to get the word out about your live shows and other public appearances. Details at events.linkedin.com.

Visit the LinkedIn Learning Center at learn.linkedin.com for a great series of tutorials on how to make the most of all that this prominent site has to offer.

#115
Make Good Use of Craigslist

Sure, people use Craigslist (www.craigslist.org) to find a job, get a date, or sell old appliances. But you can use it for your music too. Post free listings to promote your gigs, book private shows, find new band members, buy and sell used gear, and more. The nice thing about

Craigslist, compared to so many of the other social networking sites, is that you don't have to create a profile page. Just log in and post a free listing.

#116

Create a Fan-Attracting Lens on Squidoo

Squidoo (www.squidoo.com) is a popular publishing platform and community that makes it easy to create a free "lens" on the topic of choice. What's a lens? According to the site:

"Lenses are pages, kind of like flyers or signposts or overview articles, that gather everything you know about your topic of interest – and snap it all into focus. Like the lens of a camera, your perspective on something. It's a super simple, fun and powerful way to share your interests, build your online identity and credibility, and connect with new readers and friends."

I've created a couple of lenses on Squidoo and have found that they do pretty well in search results. So, this site provides another good way for fans to find you online. Great, but how should you use it?

Well, you could start a lens dedicated to your band or new album. But a better "guerrilla" idea would be to create one related to some aspect of your musical genre or a more popular artist or trend related to your style. For example, let's say you have a new album of romantic love songs. What would be a more effective lens? "Here's Info About My New Album" or "How to Use Music to Improve Your Love Life"?

I hope you agree that the second angle would be far more powerful. On such a lens you would link to your own web sites, of course. But to make it truly buzz-worthy, you would also include links to your favorite romance-related blogs, books, YouTube video clips, photos, and more. You could also include polls and other interactive features –

all designed to lure potential fans to your lens, where they will find out more about its creator: you!

#117

Use Meetup to Connect With Like-Minded People Face to Face

This web site's mission is to "revitalize local community and help people around the world self-organize." Meetup (www.meetup.com) makes it easy for anyone to organize a local group or find one of thousands already meeting face to face.

I didn't realize the power of Meetup for music marketing until I held a conference call for people who pre-ordered this book. On the phone that night was musician Loretta Hale, one of my former Berklee students from Hamilton, Ontario, Canada.

Loretta discovered that a group of 30 people who attended her band's show were there because one of them organized a group on Meetup. But the group had nothing to do with music. It was simply a club dedicated to social events in the Hamilton, Ontario, area.

Soon after, Loretta started a Meetup account and joined a couple of the bigger Hamilton-based groups. In addition, she got involved in a local hiking club because it's an activity she enjoys. And since her band, Andre & the J-Tones (www.andreandthejtones.com), plays R&B and swing dance music, she also connected with local dance-themed groups. As a result, the band is seeing greater attendance at shows.

"Meetup is a great way for us to connect with large communities of people who often come to our shows," Loretta says. "The site has lots of groups of people looking for events to go to. They love meeting the band members and getting to know us."

Sonnie Brown, host of a radio show called "SongTown" on KCBX (www.kcbx.org) in San Luis Obispo, California, was on that same conference call. She remarks, "Loretta's experience with Meetup is inspiring. I like it because it isn't *just* about promoting your music. It gets you out into your community, gets you involved with people who like a lot of different things, and helps you find a new audience for your music – while you're going hiking and doing other things you love."

Sounds like a great way to incorporate music into your life!

#118

Check Out (and "Check In" With) Location-Based Services

Ready for a new acronym? How about LBS. It stands for "location-based service." In recent years, there has been an explosion of web sites and applications that make use of geography and where people are physically located.

This trend is being fueled by the widespread use of mobile smartphones that have GPS (yet another acronym that stands for Global Positioning System) capabilities. Some practical uses of this technology take place when you use a map app to get directions or a weather app to get the local forecast. Your smartphone sends a signal to a satellite, which detects your location, and quickly feeds you the info you need based on your location.

Well, some enterprising people saw the possibilities this technology held for restaurants, bars, museums, parks, etc. This led to popular services such as **Foursquare** (www.foursquare.com) and **Gowalla** (www.gowalla.com), which allow you to "Check In" and alert your friends as to where you are and what you're doing.

SCVNGR (www.scvngr.com) is another interesting service that adds challenges and a scavenger hunt theme to where you are. Even social media giant Facebook has entered the location game with its **Facebook Places** (www.facebook.com/places) feature.

Warning: This scares some people who simply don't want everyone to know their whereabouts and every move. But don't worry. These applications let you control when you indicate where you are and who gets to see it. Just be smart and safe about it.

How to Use Location for Music Marketing

A lot of marketers are salivating at the possibilities of location-based promotion and advertising. Think about it ...

Google and others already deliver relevant ads based on the search terms you use. Search for "Pizza in Milwaukee" and you'll get an instant list of pizza places in that city. And many sites already use the location of your home computer's IP address to deliver relevant local content for your city.

Now that so many people rely on mobile phones with GPS capabilities, it only makes sense that you should get customized information based on *where you are*. But there are other aspects to this worth exploring.

For instance, when your fans publicly announce they are attending one of your live shows, that message gets broadcast to all of their friends. That's why location-based social sites and marketing delivery systems are on the rise.

Good example: Singer James Blunt promoted his album, *Some Kind of Trouble*, using Facebook Places. Fans who checked in to the venue where his CD launch party was held were rewarded with three unreleased

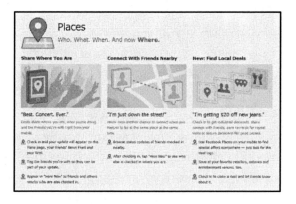

tracks. (Since the check-ins are publicly posted, it's fairly easy to discover who qualifies for the reward.) He plans to use a similar location-based tactic on his U.K. tour. Gig-goers who check in to the venues on Facebook will get access to a live version of an album track.

The band Weezer employed a similar promotion. Fans who check in to the concert venue the night of their show gets a free music download and a discounted price on their new album.

Here's another idea ...

If you have a sizeable fan base in a certain city, you might alert your fans there that you plan to give a surprise concert at an undisclosed small venue on a specific date. That day, you reveal the location and "check in" to the venue. Your most tech-savvy fans will see your status update that reveals the location, spread the word to their friends, and a nice crowd may show up for the gig.

Yes, I know it's one more thing to add to your overflowing plate. And yes, there are privacy concerns and other issues you must consider. But … I hope you can see the potential value of location-based music marketing.

#119

Get This Grab Bag of Google Goodies

No matter what you think of the almighty Google empire, you've got to admit, it's an amazing company. What started as a quick and efficient search engine in the late 1990s is now a ubiquitous international corporation that offers a wide array of online tools – most of them free.

Throughout this book, I have made references to a number of Google services, including Search, Gmail, Groups, Checkout, Translate, Blog Search, Directory, AdWords, Picasa, and Blogger. Here's a list of some other free tools available from Google that you can use for music promotion:

Google Profile
www.google.com/profiles
After you sign up for a free Google account, be sure to fill out your Google profile. Add a photo, links to your various web sites, contact info, and details about who you are in the "About me" section.

Google Buzz
www.google.com/buzz
This is Google's social networking and status update system. It doesn't have the "buzz" of Facebook and Twitter, but you might as well activate it and incorporate it into your online communications.

Google Maps

maps.google.com

Of course, you can use this popular application to get driving directions, but there's more you can do with it. For example, instead of just giving your fans the address of the venue where your next show is, give them a Google Maps link. Sure, fans can "map it" themselves. But why not save them a couple extra steps and provide a direct link?

Tip: Look up a venue address on Google Maps yourself first. Then click on "Link" (just to the right of "Print" and "Send") to get the code.

Google Calendar

www.google.com/calendar

Many people use this feature for personal appointments and scheduling. But you can also use Google Calendar to display your live show schedule. How? You can choose categories on your calendar to make public — and even embed them on your web site.

Google Voice

voice.google.com

This is a really cool feature if you want to offer a public phone contact option but don't want to use any of your personal phone numbers. Google will give you a phone number that you can have forwarded to the phone of your choice, or you can have incoming calls sent to voicemail and emailed to you. As of this writing, calls and text messages sent inside the U.S. and Canada are free, with low rates everywhere else.

Google Docs

docs.google.com

This is a great way to store important files "in the cloud." You can get to your files anywhere you have Internet access, even from your smartphone. Start a lyric and song ideas Word document. When inspiration strikes, open the file and add to it. The updated file will be waiting for you the next time you want to open it.

Cool feature: Some people use Google Docs spreadsheet forms to collect names and emails for their mailing list and special promotions.

Google Trends
www.google.com/trends

This is a great tool to find out what people are searching for and buzzing about online. Use these topics to inspire new song or blog post ideas. When done right, tapping into popular topics can act as a marketing magnet.

Google Alerts
www.google.com/alerts

This feature allows you to get email updates of the latest Google results (from web sites, news sources, blogs, and more) based on the topic or search string of your choice. You should set one up for your artist, band or company name for sure, so you know when someone has written about you. You might also create one for your genre, so you stay up to date on the latest buzz related to your musical style.

Google Friend Connect
www.google.com/friendconnect

Turn your web site into a social networking playground with Google Friend Connect. This tool makes it easy for people to join your community of fans. Choose from a range of gadgets to get users commenting, rating, sharing, etc.

Google Product Search
www.google.com/products

This service is kind of like Google's version of Ebay. It helps shoppers find and buy products across the Web. As a seller, you can submit your albums and merchandise to Google Product Search, allowing consumers to quickly and easily find you. There are no charges for uploading your items or the additional traffic you receive.

Google Reader

www.google.com/reader

Use this tool as your one-stop music education and news source. Add feeds from your favorite music blogs and news sites. Then, when you open Google Reader, you'll see all the latest posts from your favorite sources in one convenient place. (Don't forget to add my blog, podcast and YouTube video channel :-)

Picnik

www.picnik.com

Google recently purchased this service, described as a site for "Fast, easy and fun photo-editing." I've used it

to add text to images and to create logos and other cool graphics. Consider using it when designing your promotional materials.

#120

Consider These Sites to Reach More Fans

In the next section, I'll cover a wide array of music-specific sites and services. Before I wrap up this section, here's a final rundown of some general sites where you might want to have a Web presence:

- **Ning.com** – This popular site gives you the ability to create your own social networking site on the topic of your choice – complete with discussion forums and video, audio and photo capabilities, and more. Note: Ning used to be free but is now a paid service.

- **FriendFeed.com** – A great service that makes it easy to funnel all of your various online RSS feed activity (blog posts, Twitter, photos, video, audio, and more) into one place. Check out the widgets there too.

- **Tagged.com** – This site boasts more than 100 million members worldwide and 25 million monthly visitors. I haven't used it thus far, but it might be worth a peek.

- **Hi5.com** – Launched in 2003, hi5 is yet another well traveled site with more than 50 million monthly visitors and an emphasis on social entertainment for the youth market.

- **Bebo.com** – A site that "combines community, self-expression and entertainment, enabling you to consume, create, discover, curate and share digital content in entirely new ways."

- **Plaxo.com** – This one started as an online address book service, but it has branched out into a more robust networking site that encourages interaction between members.

Yes, we've covered a lot of ground already in this book. But there's one more section to go – and it's an important one that features dozens of music-specific sites and services that can help you reach the masses online.

So go to the next page and continue reading ...

Powerful Music-Specific Sites & Online Services You Need to Know About

In this fifth section we examine some of the music-specific web sites and services that exist to help independent artists promote and manage their own careers, as well as sell music and merchandise.

There seems to be more and more sites like these popping up all the time. But, at the time of this writing, the following sites were the ones most worth paying attention to.

#121

Use These Music Promotion and Sales Tools to Connect With More Fans

ReverbNation.com
www.reverbnation.com

ReverbNation is an online music-marketing platform used by more than a million artists, managers, record labels, and venues.

According to the site, the service "provides free and affordable solutions to individual artists and the music industry professionals who support them in the areas of web promotion, fan-relationship management, digital distribution, social-media marketing, direct-to-fan e-commerce, fan-behavior measurement, sentiment tracking, web-site hosting, and concert booking and promotion."

Just about all of the musicians I've talked to who use ReverbNation speak highly of it. If you promote music online, you should have an account there.

Bandcamp
www.bandcamp.com

Bandcamp is another site that offers a lot of musician friendly tools to help you sell music and merchandise. The site lists Sufjan Stevens, Amanda Palmer, and Zoë Keating among its artist users and claims to have driven nearly 800,000 paid transactions that served 12 million downloads to fans.

According to the site, "On Bandcamp, albums outsell tracks 5 to 1 (in the rest of the music buying world, tracks outsell albums 16 to 1). On name-your-price albums, fans pay an average of 50% more than whatever you set as your minimum." No wonder so many artists are happy using this service.

Topspin Media
www.topspinmedia.com

This site created a lot of buzz in recent years as a new direct-to-fan platform that gives artists and music companies a range of sales and fan relationship tools. It didn't hurt that high-profile acts like Arcade Fire, Barenaked Ladies, David Byrne, Brian Eno, Lenny Kravitz, and OK Go used the service.

Among other things, the Topspin service provides a shopping cart that can sell digital media, tickets, CDs, apparel, and other merchandise. It also allows artists to create embeddable widgets and custom audio/video streaming players linked to artist offers.

The site explains, "Topspin combines media management, fan management, distribution, sales reporting, and analytics in one environment."

Topspin started out as a closed service that was by invitation or approval only. But now the site has opened its platform to any artist or record label willing to pay a modest monthly fee.

Nimbit
www.nimbit.com

Anyone who says there are no music sales opportunities these days is delusional. Nimbit is yet another tool for music sales and fan engagement – and it's actually been around for a while. This service gives you a sales storefront that can be used on Facebook, Myspace and other sites, catalog management and soundscan reporting, and tools for messaging and tracking your fans.

In addition, Nimbit provides credit card processing, warehousing and fulfillment of physical orders; a complete web site called Instant Band Site; and digital distribution on iTunes, Amazon, Rhapsody, and other online retailers.

SoundCloud
www.soundcloud.com

This service has been growing in popularity by making it easy to upload and share audio files. SoundCloud gives users simple music widgets that can be shared, embedded, commented on, and more.

Magnatune
www.magnatune.com

John Buckman founded Magnatune as a "next-generation record label offering shared revenue, sales, and licensing to its musicians." It's a refreshing and very indie friendly business model.

The Orchard
www.theorchard.com

The Orchard describes itself as "an independent music and video distributor." More specifically, "We partner with companies of all sizes, from major independent record labels to management firms to production companies, to make their music and videos available across more than 660 digital and mobile outlets in 75 countries, as well as physical retailers across North America and Europe."

Audiolife
www.audiolife.com

Audiolife was founded in 2005 on three core pillars: technology, merchandising and fulfillment. The site serves more than 50,000 artists around the world, including Rihanna, James Taylor and Thom Yorke.

Blast My Music
www.blastmymusic.com

Another online service that lets you sell your music directly from your web site using its Music Blaster widget.

Big Cartel
www.bigcartel.com

A site that offers a simple shopping cart used by clothing designers, bands, record labels, jewelry makers, crafters, and other artists.

Loudfeed
www.loudfeed.com

This one provides embeddable sales widgets (with e-commerce by Amazon Simple Pay) and free hosting for electronic press kits.

#122

Get Organized With These Music Career Self-Management Tools

BandCentral
www.bandcentral.com

If want to get all of your music-related affairs in order, this may be the service for you. According to the web site: "BandCentral gives bands, managers and labels a suite of easy-to-use tools to help organize ... gigs and tours, band finances and release management, fan relationships and inter-team communication – all from within one central multi-login BandHub."

Bandize
www.bandize.com

Bandize is a web application that helps artists "take control of their careers by giving them an intuitive, simple way to get organized." Use this site to track tour dates, travel arrangements, income, expenses, to-do checklists, and more.

Indie Band Manager
www.indiebandmanager.com

Developed by musician Charlie Cheney, Indie Band Manager is a database software system designed to manage a performing career. Musicians, agents, labels, and publicists all over the world manage thousands of pages of information on fans, venues, media contacts, bookings, inventory, finance, content, and calendar all in one place.

Basecamp
www.basecamphq.com

Basecamp is a super simple project management system from 37signals. The company claims that the program "tackles project management [with] ... a focus on communication and collaboration. Basecamp brings people together."

Indaba Music
www.indabamusic.com

This site launched in 2007 with a simple goal in mind: to make musicians' lives easier. "We created a place for musicians around the world to network and make music together through online collaboration and have grown to over 500,000 musicians – from hobbyists to Grammy Award winners."

#123
Track Your Marketing Results With These Data and Measurement Tools

Band Metrics
www.bandmetrics.com

Musicians, bands, labels, managers, booking agencies, and venues use this service to "identify fans, measure social engagement, find hot markets, track radio plays, discover trends, gauge attitudes, and more."

RockDex
www.rockdex.com

RockDex is an online application that tracks thousands of web sites, collecting data on musical artists from blog posts, fan connections, page views, tweets, song plays, and more. Using it, you can spot viral trends and track progress over time with constantly updated charts, graphs and maps. Gauge your marketing strategy's effectiveness by finding out who your fans are, where they are, and what they're saying.

Next Big Sound
www.nextbigsound.com

This site says, "The listening, discovery, and purchase decisions of millions of consumers has moved online and the pace of this transition is only accelerating ... We believe in the power of data to transform the music industry." Next Big Sound provides a centralized place to monitor the behavior and activity of artists and bands online and off.

Perk: *Billboard* uses data from Next Big Sound to compile its new Social 50 Chart at www.billboard.com/charts/social-50.

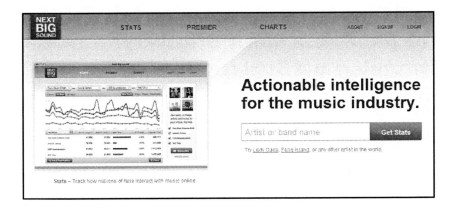

Musicmetric
www.musicmetric.com

According to the site, "We aggregate and analyze all music-related information available on the Web. From web sites mentioning an artist or release, the social networks frequented by music fans, peer-to-peer networks used to trade music, and anywhere music fans leave a comment, we aim to be there and to track the activity."

Social Mention
www.socialmention.com

This site is geared for a general audience. "Social Mention is a social media search and analysis platform that … allows you to easily track and measure what people are saying about you, your company, a new product, or any topic across the web's social media landscape in real-time. Social Mention monitors 100+ social media properties directly, including Twitter, Facebook, FriendFeed, YouTube, Digg, Google, etc."

HowSociable
www.howsociable.com

Simply put, "HowSociable provides a simple way for you to begin measuring your brand's visibility on the social web."

#124
Tap Into These Music Discovery, Streaming and Subscription Sites

iLike
www.ilike.com

iLike describes itself as "a social music discovery service … With more than 60 million registered users, iLike helps people share music recommendations, playlists, and personalized concert alerts."

Here's something that should really interest you: iLike offers musicians and labels a dashboard that helps them reach fans and manage their presence across Facebook, Google, iLike.com, iTunes, and more. Using a vast database of connections between consumers and their favorite artists, iLike helps artists reach fans and cultivate the viral spread of their music.

Last.fm
www.last.fm

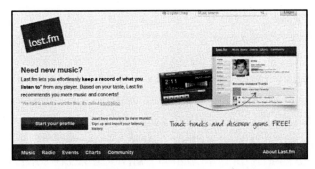

Last.fm helps music fans keep track of what they listen to and enjoy. It then suggests artists and events that each fan might also like. As the site says, "Based on your taste, Last.fm recommends more music and concerts." Sign up for an artist or label account and increase the odds that your music will be discovered by some of Last.fm's 40 million users.

Pandora
www.pandora.com

Pandora is perhaps the most widely known site in the "streaming music" category. What sets it apart is its connection to the Music Genome Project, which Pandora describes as "the most comprehensive analysis of music ever undertaken."

Since 2000, the project's "team of musician-analysts has been listening to music, one song at a time, studying and collecting literally hundreds of musical details on every track – melody, harmony, instrumentation, rhythm, vocals, lyrics, and more."

After starting a Pandora account, users can create different "stations" dedicated to a genre or artist of their choice. Based on the songs the user enters into the station playlist, Pandora then adds others songs that its Music Genome Project determines to be good matches.

You can submit your music to Pandora at submitmusic.pandora.com. Not every artist is accepted. Be sure to read the submission guidelines at blog.pandora.com/faq/contents/31.html to improve your odds.

Spotify
www.spotify.com

Spotify has been in the news a lot lately as a prime example of a new breed of "music subscription" service. It's a music streaming platform founded in Sweden that is popular in several Western European countries. Like the other sites in this section, users can create playlists and search for both well-known and obscure songs they enjoy.

Spotify offers both free accounts supported by advertising and paid subscriptions without ads that come with extra features like higher bitrate streams and offline access to music. The service reportedly has about 10 million users with over one million paying members across Europe.

There's been a lot of talk about Spotify being made available to users in the United States and other countries. The main holdup has been ironing out agreements with major music companies such as Sony, EMI, Warner Music Group, and Universal.

You can get details on how to submit your music to Spotify at www.spotify.com/int/work-with-us/labels-and-artists/. Note that the service has received criticism for not adequately compensating independent artists. So do some research and decide what's best for you.

Grooveshark
www.grooveshark.com

This is another popular music streaming and recommendation service that allows users to search for, stream, and upload music free of charge. Grooveshark reportedly streams 50 to 60 million songs per month to more than 400,000 users. Sign up for a Grooveshark Artist account at artists.grooveshark.com.

TheSixtyOne
www.thesixtyone.com

This site – named after Highway 61, a U.S. route with many links to American music culture – uses this as its motto: "On thesixtyone, new artists make music and listeners decide what's good."

More from the site: "We're nurturing a growing ecosystem where talented folks can sell songs and merchandise directly to their fans. Unlike a record or distribution deal where they only make $1-2 per album … artists on thesixtyone make at least $7 per album and are paid every 30 days – no wait for recoupment and no complex royalty schemes."

To sign up, click "login" on the lower left hand corner of the home page, then "or join" in the pop-up box. Specify that you are signing up as an "artist." After registering, go to the settings menu on the upper right and select "songs." You can now upload songs by clicking on the "add song" button. Be sure to specify background photos for each of your songs and for your artist page as well.

Jango
www.jango.com

Jango strives to make online music easy, fun and social. According to the site, "Just type in an artist and your first station starts playing right away. You'll get the music you want, along with similar favorites of Jango users who share your taste."

Note: Jango offers paid placement opportunities for indie acts and labels on the site; I couldn't find a way to submit music for free.

#125

Ask Your Fans for Financial Support Using These Fan-Funding Sites

Kickstarter
www.kickstarter.com

One of the great things about the era we live in is that the power has shifted away from major record labels and corporations. Music careers are now being directed more by artists and their fans. One result of this trend is the rise of "fan-funded" albums and other music projects whereby a number of fans contribute to an upcoming project, often in exchange for a perk of some kind.

Several services have popped up in recent years to facilitate these financial arrangements. The premier site in this category appears to be Kickstarter, which describes itself as "a new way to fund creative projects." Its philosophy: "A large group of people can be a tremendous source of money and encouragement" for musicians, filmmakers, designers, writers, illustrators, performers, and more.

Kickstarter is powered by an all-or-nothing funding method where projects must be fully funded or no money changes hands. That's why, if you start a project, be sure to choose your target dollar amount wisely. The site gives you plenty of ways to communicate your project goals: blog posts, pictures, videos, and more. The most effective Kickstarter campaigns tell stories about and by the artists themselves.

Sellaband
www.sellaband.com

This music-specific fan-funding site, based in Munich and Amsterdam, has been around since 2006. SellaBand claims that more than $3 million has been raised by indie bands and artists using the site. As with all the other sites in this category, artists retain complete ownership of the works created and have the flexibility to determine what incentives they will offer fans who fund them.

IndieGoGo
www.indiegogo.com

This site's mission is to "enable you to get your ideas funded." IndieGoGo offers anyone with an idea – creative, cause-related, or entrepreneurial – the tools to effectively build a campaign and raise money. This international service has helped raise millions of dollars for over 15,000 campaigns across 163 countries.

ChipIn
www.chipin.com

According to the web site, "ChipIn's mission is to make it easy to collect money. We enable users to organize group payments and fundraisers (called "ChipIns") in a quick, easy and secure way." The service also makes it simple for organizers to publicize their ChipIns by providing them with fundraising widgets that can be embedded on blogs and social media sites.

#126
Use These Sites to Get More Gigs

Sonicbids
www.sonicbids.com

Here's the official tagline for this service: "Sonicbids helps bands get gigs and promoters book the right bands." In my mind, Sonicbids is the premier place to host your electronic press kit (EPK).

While you can create an EPK yourself on your own web site, this service offers a simple place to host your bio, photos, audio and video content, set list, media links, calendar, and more … for the primary purpose of landing gigs and slots at festivals and other music events. Fees range from $6 to $11 per month, plus additional fees when you submit to certain event listings.

Indie on the Move
www.indieonthemove.com

From the web site: "The creators of this site include original members of the rock band ZELAZOWA, who in just three years performed over 500 shows internationally without the aid of a booking agent, band manager, record label, or any other industry professional. It is our mission to help you do the same." The site is primarily a music venue database that artists, fans, agents, labels, venues, and promoters are encouraged to rate and review – for free.

Concerts In Your Home
www.concertsinyourhome.com

Use this site to find hundreds of house concert "hosts" who regularly bring music into their home. A great resource!

House Concert / Listening Room Directory
www.houseconcerts.com/venue.php

A concise listing of house concert venues and hosts.

Eventful
www.eventful.com

Eventful has nearly 15 million registered members who use the site to discover, promote, share, and create events. A unique thing about Eventful is its "Demand it" feature, which allows fans to request that their favorite artist perform live in a specific area. Musicians can use this data to make informed decisions about where to tour.

GigMaven

www.gigmaven.com

This is a free service based in New York City that helps musicians and live music venues book gigs online.

BetterThanTheVan

www.betterthanthevan.com

Use this site to find free places to stay in the US, Canada and Europe; host shows, bands, and other music minded travelers; and directly connect with venues, fans and friends.

Gig Salad

www.gigsalad.com

Gig Salad is an online resource that connects event planners with entertainment and party vendors. The site offers both free and paid memberships that allow you to create an artist profile that can be viewed by people looking for entertainment.

Gig Masters

www.gigmasters.com

This site offers various paid membership levels that can connect you with people booking music for private parties, weddings, corporate events, and more.

#127

Create and Sell Music Merchandise Using These Services

CafePress
www.cafepress.com

Self-described as "The world's favorite place to find or make unique T-shirts and gifts," CafePress offers an easy way to create on-demand products emblazoned with your band or company logo, song lyrics, etc. The site boasts more than 10 million unique visitors per month.

Zazzle
www.zazzle.com/music

Similar to CafePress, Zazzle is another prominent service in the on-demand merchandise category. After opening an account, you can upload your artwork and have it printed on T-shirts, hats, coffee mugs, keychains, and a lot more – including greeting cards and calendars.

Stickersandmore
www.stickersandmore.com

Services like CafePress and Zazzle are easy merchandise options with no set-up fees or inventory investment. But frankly, they aren't very profitable for most artists, because the cost per item is relatively high. To make decent money with merch, you'll need to produce things in quantity. One good source for that is Stickersandmore, an indie friendly service that can print T-shirts, posters, business cards, buttons, magnets, stickers, and ... well ... more.

Printfection
www.printfection.com

Printfection is described as "an all-in-one merchandise fulfillment service. From your own online storefront to printing, fulfillment and customer service, we make it easy to launch a killer merchandising program."

Spreadshirt
www.spreadshirt.com

This is yet another site that creates on-demand merchandise.

#128

Tap Into the Power of These Helpful Music Sites and Services

SoundExchange
www.soundexchange.com

SoundExchange is the non-profit performance rights organization that collects statutory royalties from satellite radio (such as SIRIUS XM), Internet radio, cable TV music channels, and similar platforms that stream sound recordings. SoundExchange is the sole entity in the United States that collects and distributes digital performance royalties on behalf of recording artists, master rights owners (like record labels), and independent artists who record and own their masters. If your music is being streamed, register now.

Brown Paper Tickets
www.brownpapertickets.com

This company refers to itself as "The fair-trade ticketing company." Think of Brown Paper Tickets as a grassroots, budget-friendly version of Ticketmaster or Live Nation. Create an event and sell tickets to it online – no matter how small or large the venue or audience. This site's philosophy: "Give more. Take less. We mean it. Turns out you don't need to charge an arm and a leg to deliver top-of-line services and exceptional support."

Eventbrite
www.eventbrite.com

This site's mission is to "empower event organizers to become more efficient and effective when bringing people together … We believe that anyone  can be an event organizer. That's why we've created tools that make it easy to sell tickets to all kinds of events – whether it's a photography class or a sold-out concert … With Eventbrite, organizers can create a customizable event page; spread the word with social media; collect money; and gain visibility …"

Creative Commons
www.creativecommons.org

Many artists want to protect their intellectual property and dislike the cultural trend of digital file sharing. But other artists embrace the way that consumers and music fans share new songs they have discovered. Creative Commons is a nonprofit organization that provides a new set of copyright licenses and tools that make it easier for content creators to share their work in a variety of ways without the constraints of "all rights reserved."

If you give your music a clearly stated Creative Commons license, it may increase the chances that bloggers, podcasters, reviewers, and others will use it and share it with other people.

#129

Consider These Additional Music Destination Sites

As if you didn't already have enough web sites to consider putting your music on ... there are more. Here's a final list of sites that could potentially connect you with active music fans:

Broadjam
www.broadjam.com

dmusic
www.dmusic.com

Jamendo
www.jamendo.com

MP3.com
www.mp3.com

OurStage
www.ourstage.com

PureVolume
www.purevolume.com

SoundClick
www.soundclick.com

Final Thoughts ...

Your Internet Music Promotion Challenge

Congratulations on investing your time and energy into reading this book and absorbing the many ideas and resources contained in it. By doing so, you have already set yourself apart from the majority of music people who don't appreciate the true value of education and personal development.

But you haven't reached the finish line yet!

There's an unfortunate curse that afflicts people who read books, attend workshops, and invest in resources like this one. I'm talking about the wide gap that often exists between the "knowing" of things and the "doing" of things. Learning this stuff is a crucial first step. But the only factor that brings it to life is *action*. That's right, now you have move all of these great ideas from the realm of thought to the very real world of substance!

My Challenge to You

Now that you've read this book and have absorbed all 129 guerrilla music marketing tactics, I encourage you to start putting some of them into practice. Then, let me know the successes and challenges you experience while implementing them. And I'm going to give you some great ways to do that, while also sharing your music promotion journey with other active musicians, managers, publicists, and readers of this book.

But first, the challenge ...

In the Next Seven Days …

Pick at least three ideas from the book and implement them right away. Strike while your interest and resolve are high. *Take action now!* Treat yourself to some mini successes in the short term to fuel your motivation for the long term.

Steps you can take in the next week include:

- **Start a free fan email list** (if you don't offer one already). Sign up for one of the email management services listed in Tip #6 and get familiar with sign-up forms, delivery options, etc.

- **Beef up your personal music web site** (or start one, if you don't yet have a site). Look over the web site tips in Section Two and tweak the design and text so it attracts your ideal type of fan.

- **Set aside time every day or two to read artist blogs, listen to podcasts, and watch music video clips**. Become an informed consumer of these formats so you have a better idea of how to use them yourself for promotion.

Here are more steps you can potentially take in the weeks and months ahead:

In the Next 30 Days …

- **Start artist accounts at CD Baby, ReverbNation, Bandcamp, Sonicbids**, and any other music-specific sites that caught your eye while reading this book.

- **Open free accounts on Facebook and Twitter**. Spend time filling out the various sections of your profile so people know who you are, what you sound like, and what sets you and your music apart.

- **Claim your name on as many social media and music sites as possible**. You may not have the time to fully work all the web sites mentioned in this book, but you should at least grab as many customized URLs as you can. You ideally want to be found at Twitter.com/yourname, Facebook.com/yourname, YouTube.com/yourname, and so on.

- **Make sure the ordering and sign-up process is clear on your web site**. Do you make it easy for people to purchase your music and get on your mailing list? Include a "call to action."

- **Reach out to bloggers, podcasters and journalists who cover your specific genre**. Compliment them, introduce yourself, and start relationships with them.

In the Next 90 Days ...

- **Make sure you are staying on top of your previous music promotion activities**: sending email updates to your fan list, researching your music genre, updating your status and interacting on Facebook and Twitter (or whatever it is that you set in motion previously).

- **Make your song downloads available for sale on iTunes** and other online music stores using CD Baby, TuneCore, or another digital music aggregator.

- **Enroll your albums in the Amazon Advantage Program or use CreateSpace** (if they're not already distributed to Amazon via another source), then register for an Amazon Artist Central profile.

- **Start free accounts at YouTube, LinkedIn, Flickr, Squidoo**, and as many popular social networking sites as time allows. Make the effort to completely fill out your profile pages on each.

- **Start a blog, if you don't already publish one**. Go to either Blogger, Posterous or Wordpress and start a free account. Then get busy posting something new every week about your musical activities.

In the Next Six Months ...

- **Take time to assess your progress over the past three months**. What has worked for you? What hasn't worked? Why? What can you do better?

- **Start your own podcast and/or start posting short video clips related to your music**. Encourage people to share the links with their friends.

- **Combine your online efforts with your real-world activities**. At live shows, collect names and email addresses and make people aware of your address on the Web. Use your Web presence and the various event web sites listed in Tips #49 and #50 to promote your live shows.

- **Learn more about RSS feeds** and how to cross-pollinate your blog posts, photos, videos, and text updates onto multiple web sites automatically.

- **Keep chipping away at it** and continue to be an evangelist for your music. Spread your message online by any ethical and authentic means you can imagine.

Now Report Your Progress

Don't promote your music in a vacuum. I want you to share your experiences with me and other music people who are on this same marketing journey.

Here are the best ways to connect:

- **Send an email to <u>bob@thebuzzfactor.com</u>** and let me know how you did following the advice in this book. Tell me what worked for you and what didn't. Also include any detailed tips you'd like to share with other artists and managers. I'll include the best stories I receive in my free *Buzz Factor* ezine and my Music Promotion Blog (which you can subscribe to for free at <u>www.TheBuzzFactor.com</u> and <u>www.MusicPromotionBlog.com</u>, respectively).

- **Like my Facebook fan page and follow me on Twitter** at <u>www.facebook.com/BobBakerFanPage</u> and <u>www.twitter.com/MrBuzzFactor</u>. Share your ideas on these forums too.

- **Join my Music Marketing Mentorship Program for ongoing advice, encouragement and inspiration**. The program features a variety of levels to suit your needs. Benefits include a subscription to my *Guerrilla Music Marketing Confidential* newsletter for members only; access to exclusive monthly audio interviews with successful artists and marketing experts; a monthly Music Mastermind conference call with me and special guests; as well as one-on-one private coaching and guidance. Details at <u>www.TheBuzzFactor.com</u>.

Stay Savvy With These Music Resources

Here are several blogs I recommend you read for ongoing marketing advice:

Hypebot
<u>www.hypebot.com</u>

Music Think Tank
<u>www.musicthinktank.com</u>

The DIY Musician Blog
diymusician.cdbaby.com

MicControl
www.miccontrol.com

Artist House Music
www.artistshousemusic.org

The Lefsetz Letter
www.lefsetz.com/wordpress

Ariel Hyatt's Blog
www.arielpublicity.com/blog

Derek Siver's Blog
www.sivers.org/blog

David Hooper's Blog
www.musicmarketing.com

Musicians Cooler
www.musicianscooler.com

Seth Godin's Blog
sethgodin.typepad.com

Scott Ginsberg's Blog
hellomynameisscott.blogspot.com

Copyblogger
www.copyblogger.com

You now have an arsenal of Internet music promotion tools at your disposal. Now go forth and put them to use!

There's no denying the opportunities that exist for you to make a splash, make a difference, and make money with your music. And there's no shortage of useful tools at your disposal – many of which are free.

The only question that remains is …

How Will You Put Them to Use?

I wish you an abundance of success, and I look forward to hearing about your progress as you successfully promote and sell your music online.

-Bob

Special Recognition Section

I like to practice what I preach, so I often promote my books and myself as an author using the very same tactics I recommend for musicians.

When I launched this book, I used my own version of the "fan funding" method. I starting selling access to the book's content before it was completely written, designed and printed. And I gave special perks to those who ordered it in advance.

(I encourage you to expand your thinking in the same way and consider new ways you can write, record, produce, promote, and share your music with your fans.)

I want to thank the following people who were brave enough to take me up on my pre-publication offer. I applaud and recognize them for playing an important role in the success of this book!

Massimo de Majo - www.visualcv.com/massimodemajo

Adrian Killens (Aidy) - www.Aidy.com

Bird Stevens - www.bird-stevens.com

Giorgio Costantini - www.pianopianoforte.com

Joe Stopka

Janne Maarala Music House - www.jannemaarala.com

Spiderhousepr - www.spiderhousepr.com

Tu Tone - www.tutone222.com

Dying Giraffe Recordings - www.dgrmusic.com

FeelAbouT - www.feelabout.com

YENN - www.yennmusic.com

The Viral Gigs System - www.viralgigs.com

Davidsony - www.davidsony.com

Eva Dowd - www.evadowdproductions.com

Grit PR & Promotion - www.gritpr.com

Colby O'Donis - www.myspace.com/iconrecords

Curt Potter - www.myspace.com/curtpotter

Van Buchanan - www.vanbuchanan.com

Bruce Nelson - www.camelhumpmusic.com

Conor Ebbs - www.conorebbs.com

Jason Ayres - www.jasonayres.com

Musicians Gazette - www.musiciansgazette.com

Ian Narcisi - www.ianmusic.com

Gordon Rivers - www.agonysoultrader.co.uk

Steven Cravis - www.stevencravis.com

Hank Wagner - www.coyotelovemusic.com

Daniele Santini - www.tibprod.com/italy

Nathan Clay - www.nathanclay.net

Inner City Groove Music - www.innercitygroove.com

Crater Rock Music, LLC - www.craterrockmusic.com

La Grua - www.lagrua.com.mx

Terri Langerak - www.harpsinger.net

Pete Cohan - www.RouteRecords.com

JJ Biener - www.jjbiener.com

Visionary Music - www.visionarymusic.com

Octobre's Ending - www.octobresending.com

Capt'n Black's Sea Dogs - www.seadogsmusic.com

Little Johnny Trailer Trash - www.littlejohnnytrailertrash.com

Black Kat Benders - www.reverbnation.com/blackkatbenders

Roland Berti - www.rolandberti.com

Kevin Downing's Guitar School - www.guitar.co.nz

Soulpajamas - www.soulpajamas.com

Bruce Danna - www.brucedanna.com

Carlos Villalobos - www.carlosvillalobos.com

Lynette Yetter - www.musicandes.com

Daily Concert Deals - www.yiplee.com

Darrin Churchill - www.darrinchurchill.com

The Caning - www.reverbnation.com/thecaning

Charlotte Mielziner

The Spiral Sequence - www.myspace.com/thespiralsequence

Rev. Roy D. Fisher - Contemporary Spiritual Arts, Inc.

Troker Mexican Jazz Band - www.troker.com.mx

Mike Monday - www.mikemonday.com

Anne Roos - www.celticharpmusic.com

Georges Poropat - www.myspace.com/analogpower

SORROWSEED - www.sorrowseed.com

VERUSIVE - www.verusive.com

Cyd Ward - www.cydward.com

Thea Kearney - www.theamusic.com

Sarana VerLin - www.saranaverlin.com

Debra Alexander - www.wordmavenmusic.com

Suzannah Doyle Music - www.suzdoyle.com

Cinthia Van de Kamp - www.facadasuamusicaumnegocio.com

LOOSE RECORDS & MUSIC - www.looserecords.com

TrackHustle.com - www.trackhustle.com

Christopher Morgan

Cynthia Shelhart - www.cynthiashelhart.com

Bran 7 - www.myspace.com/bran913

Moonwalk - www.moonwalk.ee

artistED - www.artisted.com

Chris Martins - www.masterguitarplaying.com

LaJuana Murphy-Brann - www.lajuanamurphy-brann.com

Trip Poppies - www.trippoppies.com

7Envy website - www.7envyband.com

Jerry Schickling - www.jerrycountry.com

MarkSchoots - www.markschoots.nl

Bri-anne Swan - www.bri-anneswan.com

BJ Nash - badfish97@live.com

Christian Calcatelli - www.solo-piano.com

Chuck Hughes - www.hillbillyhellcats.com

Ben Coulter's Country Music - www.bencoulteronline.com

Kathena Bryant - www.thehippynuts.com

Tranquilizer Records - www.tranquilizerrecords.com

Danica Thomas - www.danicathomas.com

Michelle Gold - www.michellegold.com

Eden Kai - www.edenkai.com

Apryl Peredo - www.interidoru.com

Will Makower - www.willmakower.com

Bill McBirnie - www.extremeflute.com

Sarah Mitchell - www.sarahmitchell.biz

Weston James - www.westonjamesmusic.com

Nicole Weitzmann

Bill McBirnie - www.extremeflute.com

Heidi McKee - www.heidimckee.net

Jerry P - www.ddandjerryp.com

Liquid Girlfriend - www.liquidgirlfriend.com

Harder Promotions - www.harderpromotions.net

Scarlet Season - www.scarletseason.com

Pragmatic Audio - www.PragmaticAudio.com

DealJay Production - www.dealjay.com

Malindia Shoptaw - www.reverbnation.com/malindiashoptawsongwriter

Bird Stevens - www.bird-stevens.com

Jessica Paige - www.jessicapaige.com

Wil Mullen - www.wilmullen.com

Christine A Rose

Jessica Caylyn Band - www.jessicacaylyn.com

LaZae - www.lazaemusic.com

Alain Pernot - www.alainpernot.com

Augean Stable - www.myspace.com/augean

Peter Weis - www.peterweis.com

Henk Wieman - www.modestmusic.eu

The Polite Jazz Quartet

Aimee Ricca - www.8waystosunday.com

Paulie Gwap - www.planetgwap.com

Denise Jones - www.royaltyandiamondgospelrecords.com

G-RILLO - www.g-rillo.com

Planet Joy - www.planetjoy.co.za

In The Cinema - www.inthecinemamusic.com

Sonnie Brown - www.sonniebrown.com

Waxwork - www.waxwork.ca

Mike Watson - www.mwswatson.com

JOANPi - www.joanpi.virb.com

Jenna's Revenge - www.jennasrevenge.co.uk

Anthony Hopp - www.anthonyhopp.com

Rohn Bailey

Rhon Van Erman - www.rhonvanerman.com

Andre & the J-Tones Rhythm & Blues Experience - www.andreandthejtones.com

MaryRose Varo - www.maryrosevaro.com

Gary Johnson - www.introspectmusicgroup.com

Holman Autry Band - www.holmanautryband.com

Fabian Holland - www.fabianholland.com

KYMYSTRY - www.kymystry.com

Larry E. Cowsert - www.12barproductions.com

Micky Small - www.mickysmall.com

Chin's Mojo - www.chinsmojo.com

Cari Cole - www.caricole.com

Ricardo Dominguez - www.newboleros.com

Doug & Sandy McMaster - www.mcmasterslackkey.com

Mikey Long - www.reasonyband.com

Steve & Joanne Scott - www.morningsongproductions.com

RecordMyDemos.com - www.recordmydemos.com

Marc Imboden - www.marcimboden.com

WP BandThemes - www.wpbandthemes.com

Stephen J King - www.chocandor.com

Rick Slagter - www.ricksrommelhok.nl

Leanne Regalla - www.leregalla.com

Hairstonning Music, LLC - www.vernonhairston.com

Rene Patrique - www.RenePatrique.com

My Pure Karma - www.mypurekarma.com

Maxine Brown - www.themaxinebrown.com

Austin Matthews

Charlie Andrew - www.charlieandrew.com

Kenneth Laufer - www.myspace.com/KenLaufer

Qwiet - www.qwiet.com

The Groves - www.thegrovesmusic.net

Soren Bogelund - www.sorenbogelund.com

Cha Cahyadi - www.chacahyadi.com

G.E.T. Phresh Entertainment Enterprises Inc. - www.getphreshent.com

Antonio Pontarelli - www.antoniomusic.com

Eden Kai - www.edenkai.com

Peter Woolston - www.peterwoolston.com

Steve Scott - www.morningsongproductions.com

Bridgette Perdue - www.bridgetteperdue.com

Jeff McCullough - www.musicproducer4hire.com

Daniel Halen - www.danielhalen.com

Mark Christian Lee - www.markchristianlee.com

Meet the Austrians - www.meettheaustrians.com

The Franklin Girls - www.majalamedia.com

Tom Hacker Music

Ken Eichler - www.kenstunes.com

Carla DeFraine - www.icarus.com

Sidewalk Dave - www.sidewalkdave.com

Debbie Corradini - www.debbiecorradini.com

Ann Parenti - www.forgottensongproductions.com

Dave Blair - www.daveblairmusic.com

John P. Sinek - www.longblacknight.com

Jerry Jennings Band - www.jerryjenningsmusic.com

Rhyme Or Reason – www.rhymeorreasonmusic.com

Doug Andrews - www.doug-andrews.net

Gil Hager - www.reverbnation.com/mojoremedy

Nfamous - www.twitter.com/iparticipate2

Bobby Martin - www.bobbymartin.com

Marc Francoeur - www.marcfrancoeur.com

John Parker - www.jparkermusic.com

October Rage - www.octoberrage.com

Anthony Fernandez - Pro Audio Nerds

Mike Fleming – www.westcoastvideo.net

Bruce Twiddy - Power Music Management

Roger Gilpin

Rusty Lavigne

Michael Collins

Scott Solberg

John Grover

Brandon Cummings

Wendy Watts

Rich Friedland

Ong Lee

Warren Lankford

James Coleman

James Jones

Ave Topel

Harvey Yates

Jay VerHoef

Turbo-Charge Your Music Career With ...

Bob Baker's Music Marketing Mentorship Program

The program includes a variety of levels to suit your needs ...

Basic – This is Bob's entry level program for self-promoting artists, managers, publicists, etc. It features a subscription to the *Guerrilla Music Marketing Confidential* newsletter, filled with Bob's latest strategies, success stories, and music trends – for members only.

Silver – This tier was created for music entrepreneurs who are ready to take their careers to the next level – and are interested in interacting with other like-minded, ambitious music people. It features a monthly Music Mastermind & Brainstorming conference call with Bob, other program members, and special guests. Plus members-only access to exclusive, full-length MP3 audio interviews with successful artists, authors and thought leaders. Also includes a subscription to *Guerrilla Music Marketing Confidential*.

Gold – When you're ready for one-on-one private coaching and guidance, the Gold Level is for you. Here you get up to 45 minutes of Bob's undivided attention every month via video Skype sessions or telephone. Get direct personalized marketing advice and inspiration on an ongoing basis. PLUS get all the benefits of a Silver Level membership above.

Platinum – If you are really serious about getting personal coaching (and acting on the strategies) this level may be for you. You'll get up to two and a half hours of Bob's undivided attention every month – a much more in-depth dose of marketing advice and inspiration on an ongoing basis. PLUS all the benefits of a Silver Level membership.

Visit **www.TheBuzzFactor.com** for more details!